The U.S. Secretaries of Education

The U.S. Secretaries of Education

A Short History of Their Lives and Impact

Catherine L. Sommervold

ROWMAN & LITTLEFIELD
Lanham • Boulder • New York • London

Published by Rowman & Littlefield
An imprint of The Rowman & Littlefield Publishing Group, Inc.
4501 Forbes Boulevard, Suite 200, Lanham, Maryland 20706
www.rowman.com
86-90 Paul Street, London EC2A 4NE, United Kingdom

Copyright © 2023 by Catherine L. Sommervold

All rights reserved. No part of this book may be reproduced in any form or by any electronic or mechanical means, including information storage and retrieval systems, without written permission from the publisher, except by a reviewer who may quote passages in a review.

British Library Cataloguing in Publication Information Available

Library of Congress Cataloging-in-Publication Data

Names: Sommervold, Catherine, 1969– author.
Title: The U.S. secretaries of education : a short history of their lives and impact / Catherine L. Sommervold.
Other titles: United States secretaries of education
Description: Lanham, Maryland : Rowman & Littlefield, 2023. | Includes bibliographical references. | Summary: "U.S. Secretaries of Education: A Short History of Their Lives and Impact by Catherine L. Sommervold is a new approach to examining education history. This book contains a short biography of each Secretary of Education and details about their tenure. The author attempts to be objective with the hope to encourage critical thinking and conversations about education and education policy"— Provided by publisher.
Identifiers: LCCN 2023015763 (print) | LCCN 2023015764 (ebook) | ISBN 9781475847987 (cloth) | ISBN 9781475847994 (paperback) | ISBN 9781475848069 (epub)
Subjects: LCSH: United States. Department of Education—Officials and employees—Biography. | United States. Department of Education—History. | Cabinet officers—United States—Biography. | Education and state—United States—History.
Classification: LCC LB2807 .S66 2023 (print) | LCC LB2807 (ebook) | DDC 353.80973—dc23/eng/20230418
LC record available at https://lccn.loc.gov/2023015763
LC ebook record available at https://lccn.loc.gov/2023015764

To Dr. Robert J. Brown. Dr. Brown believed in the power of partnerships and collaboration. His passion for the community led me to this topic. The stories that he shared about the politics surrounding the Department of Education were fascinating. This hearsay supported by news reports and education articles helped build a profile of each secretary. He was always supportive, enthusiastic, and had a story to share. The world is not quite as bright without him. Finishing this book seems like the best thing I can do to honor his memory. RIP Dr. Bob.

Contents

Preface	ix
Acknowledgments	xiii
Introduction	xv
Chapter 1: Shirley M. Hufstedler: 1979–1981	1
Chapter 2: Terrel Bell: 1981–1985	7
Chapter 3: William J. Bennett: 1985–1988	15
Chapter 4: Lauro F. Cavazos, Jr.: 1988–1990	21
Chapter 5: Lamar Alexander: 1991–1993	27
Chapter 6: Richard Riley: 1993–2001	33
Chapter 7: Rod Paige: 2001–2005	39
Chapter 8: Margaret Spellings: 2005–2009	45
Chapter 9: Arne Duncan: 2009–2016	49
Chapter 10: John King, Jr.: 2016–2017	55
Chapter 11: Elizabeth "Betsy" DeVos: 2017–2021	59
Chapter 12: Miguel Cardona: 2021–present	65
Chapter 13: The Acting Secretaries: Ted Sanders (1990–1991), Phil Rosenfelt (January–February 2017 and January–March 2021), and Mick Zais (January 2021)	71

Conclusion	75
Appendix: The U.S. Secretaries of Education, 1979–present	77
References	79

Preface

This book began as a conversation between a doctoral student and adviser. Time and life circumstances led it to be put on the back burner for a decade and a half, but here it is. When looking at education, the challenge becomes how to exclude things. So many pieces of policy and standards are relevant that staying focused on just the secretaries, to tell their stories, became difficult. It is also necessary.

This is, as far as could be found, the first and only book about the secretaries of education. Which is somewhat surprising. The secretary of education is part of the president's cabinet and could, possibly, if things go terribly wrong, act as commander in chief of the United States. It seems prudent to know who has been in that seat and what has happened. Some of it is standard bill-passing politics.

But some of the history is much more interesting. The people who have served are accomplished people who come with a myriad of experiences from a variety of backgrounds. As education continues to be politicized as part of the national conversation and has become a key piece of campaign platforms, people need to pay attention.

Every person has some piece of information or opinion about it, even if that piece is small. Of the things humans experience in this world, education is ubiquitous. Everyone has experience with education—as a student, parent, or someone affiliated with a school at some level. It is interesting that only 8–10% of the education budget for each state comes from the federal government: the rest is from state and local taxes and funding. How does a player that contributes so little get to mandate so much, and who is in charge of the ship?

The question might be asked, "What prompts a person who teaches leadership and doctoral studies—and has written books on critical thinking and creativity and moral imagination—to dive into history, especially contemporary political history?" Philosophically, the idea that how political decisions are made and what is needed from leadership sit at the intersection of history and theory; there cannot be one without the other.

The process of using moral imagination as a decision-making process focuses on creative problems solving relative to antecedent events and both short and long term consequences. The understanding of how future events relate to past outcomes is history. Politics and education are fascinating: all of it—especially the mechanics of how things become national acts and laws. From watching *School House Rock*'s, "I'm Just a Bill," to studying state senates, bills, lobbying, and reviewing red herring sound bites, there is interest in how the actions that take place in the name of policy impact our daily lives.

It is important to examine the trajectory of those who lead us and ask whether they do *actually* lead us or if they are merely figureheads. The fact that the Department of Education is relatively new (1979) and that there have been so few secretaries of education may be another reason this topic is so compelling. As it has not been around since the inception of the cabinet, people forget to consider the secretary of education.

My family has always emphasized the idea that if "one did not participate, one did not get to complain." The best way to change something is from the inside; it is why I became involved in education. Even so, from a policy standpoint, I am still on the outside looking in at the political machine. As someone who has been involved in education, as a student, parent, or instructor, for the last (yikes) 45 years, I believe more consideration needs to go into who is in control of our schools and what they are facing as they try to navigate budgets and media coverage.

The goal of this book is to present a brief biography of each secretary, give a taste of the general political climate during which he or she served and highlight the acts that were passed during each tenure. I hope that the way in which this information is presented will encourage critical thinking around who is in charge and how they got there. Hopefully patterns or trends will present themselves. It is valuable to look at our history from various perspectives. Patterns or themes can emerge that were not obvious until information is pulled together in one place.

My hope is that this book will be used by a variety of people and in a variety of ways; that it can be a tool that presents information that allows people to examine it from different angles and think about it critically. Finally, this book should increase awareness about the people and policies that directly impact our schools and the billions of dollars that are associated with the department.

The information provided in these pages was retrieved from books, archives, articles, and periodicals: both hard copy and digital. The portrayals of the secretaries relied heavily on journal articles, trade summaries, and government websites. The bias of those sources should be taken into account when questioning the information. Historical scholar John Tosh states, "The archive is not just a record of government; it is an instrument of the government, and the accuracy of its records is skewed by administrative priorities and prejudices" (Tosh, 2015). This is true of all history; it is authored by people who are influenced by the world around them.

With regard to the criteria by which materials were selected, I relied on instinct and as Lewis Namier suggests, "The function of the historian is akin to that of a painter and not the photographic camera: to discover and set forth to single out and stress that which is of the nature of the things, and not to reproduce indiscriminately all that meets the eye" (Tosh, 2015).

This book will not examine or voice opinions on the policies or acts at hand—as an example, there will be no judgment of NCLB or privatization and will state the focus of each secretary based on what is discovered. While there is no intent to let obvious bias show, there is no guarantee that some biases will not raise their heads a little. Regardless, the point remains: use this book as a tool for dialogue.

In nature the only time things reach equilibrium is when they are dead. Politics, education, policy . . . schools—all are very much alive, which means they are never static. Perspectives should be collected from all who are served to see how our schools best move forward and ensure literacy. How is it measured if the goal of education in the United States has evolved? Has moved forward since where it began? Knowledge and education are, in antiquated terms, "the great equalizers." As Thomas Jefferson stated in his Bill for the More General Diffusion of Knowledge,

> [E]xperience hath shewn, that even under the best forms, those entrusted with power have, in time, and by slow operations, perverted it into tyranny; and it is believed that the most effectual means of preventing this would be, to illuminate, as far as practicable, the minds of the people at large, and more especially to give them knowledge of those facts, which history exhibiteth, that, possessed thereby of the experience of other ages and countries, they may be enabled to know ambition under all its shapes, and prompt to exert their natural powers to defeat its purposes. (Jefferson, 1779)

While not provided for in the Constitution, education has always been included in our political structure to educate our citizens through a combination of local public and private means. If we do not provide the opportunity for an educated populace, we are hobbling the citizens of this country. Our freedom lies in our ability to access, interpret, understand, and share information. This book presents an overview of what the people who are/have been in charge of the decisions that fund these opportunities are doing to make sure that continues to happen.

Acknowledgments

Thank you to my family who endured the crazy writing patterns and weird idiosyncrasies that accompany writing around working, researching, parenting, and life. It's normal to have a "writing coffee cup," right? I love that my household of men are always my best cheerleaders.

I would also like to thank Dr. Robert J. Brown for the ideas, stories, and encouragement; Tom Koerner and Carlie Wall for their patience and support; and Doane University for encouraging and supporting scholarship within their faculty.

Introduction

> *The United States has the most complicated constitutional and political system to be found anywhere in the world. Our Founding Fathers deliberately made it that way to protect our individual liberties from those who govern.*
>
> —Dean Rusk, 54th Secretary of State

In a letter titled, "Open Letter to a Cabinet Member," dated January 11, 1981, outgoing Secretary of Education Shirley Hufstedler gave words of advice to incoming Secretary of Education Terrel Bell. Hufstedler summarized the conflicting interests of the position,

> [Y]ou must contend with hundreds of interest groups, ranging from advocates for more sex education to those who are horrified at what children are already being taught. All the while, you must obey, simultaneously, the President, the Congress and the courts—even when they are moving in different directions. And you must explain to the nation, through the media, what it is that you are doing and why on earth it is necessary. (Hufstedler, 1981)

Hufstedler's words are as true today as they were in 1981. The Department of Education and those in its employ are pulled in a myriad of directions. Education has been highly politicized since the federal government was allowed to determine how funds were allocated (Ravitch, 1983) and it has remained so. Whether constituents like it or not, education is a focal point in American politics.

In summer 2022, a quick survey of the Take Action section on the National Education Association (NEA) website included topics such as "Ban Assault Weapons," "Pass the Respect for Marriage Act," "Take Action Today to Support Title IX," and "Invest in School Meals and the People Who Prepare Them" (NEA, 2022). Mainstream news, such as *USA Today*, frequently covers educational issues. As of this writing, a quick search of their website for *education* pulls up items regarding teacher pay, allowing military spouses to teach without credentials, an antisemitic logo in Georgia, and how early reading skills can impact your child's future (U.S. News, 2022).

It is interesting to see how education moved from discussions about an independent education department to where it is today. Context is critical to contemporary education conversations—some believe education uses antiquated measures in a contemporary context. While education policy and history books often cover government initiatives, they rarely include background and information on the people who are the leaders during the times of the initiatives and discussions.

The purpose of this book is to explore the impact of each secretary of education on national education and educational trends. Beginning with the first organized school in Massachusetts to an office with a $188 billion budget in an industry with a market valued at $1.1 trillion in 2021 (Zion Market Research, 2022), education plays a significant role in the U.S. economy and policy.

As the tenure of each secretary is reviewed, the impact of global and national politics on educational policy may become evident. This is not meant to be a positive or negative comment on the department; this book is meant to simply outline the evolution and impact our secretaries and their decisions have had on how U.S. students experience public education through a brief overview of their tenure.

THE CABINET

Cabinet members are not required or provided for in the U.S. Constitution. In fact, no law says that the president must have a cabinet, the Constitution only says that the president "may require the opinion, in writing of the principal officer in each of the executive departments, upon any subject relating to the duties of the respective offices" (U.S. Constitution, 1776). Presidents are allowed a group of official advisors.

George Washington began with a four-person cabinet: the secretary of state, the secretary of treasury, the secretary of war, and the attorney general (Parker, 1978). James Madison was the first to use the term *cabinet* and it has been used ever since (White House, 2022). While not required, cabinet members are appointed; they are chosen with the "advice and consent" of the senate (Parker, 1978).

The U.S. cabinet continues to grow, and positions are added as national needs dictate. In 1913, the number of cabinet seats was eight until it began to grow again 40 years later in 1953, when the Department of Health, Education, and Welfare (later to become Health and Welfare in 1980 when Education was pulled out in 1979) was added.

In January 1977, Jimmy Carter was sworn in as the 39th president of the United States. During Carter's presidency he added two cabinet-level positions to the executive branch of the U.S. government. Carter added a secretary of energy in 1977, and then in 1978 he added an additional position, the secretary of education (Parker, 1978). In 2022, the secretary of education was the 13th person in line for the presidency and one of 15 people in the president's cabinet.

Prior to a cabinet-level position, education matters were housed under the Department of Health, Education, and Welfare and had over 160 programs housed in various departments. The creation of a cabinet-level education position had been discussed and presented to the Congress before. Between 1908 and 1975 there were more than 130 bills introduced to form a Department of Education (Stallings, 2002). "Despite concerns about an overt federalization of education, locating all of the disparate programs into a single, separate office and giving it department status became the rallying cry of a small but growing minority from as early as the Reconstruction period" (Stallings, 2002).

During President Carter's term as president, with Carter's support and the predominance of the National Education Association (NEA), the creation of a cabinet-level department was made possible. In fact, Carter advocated for a stand-alone department in his 1976 campaign. The 1976 election was a turning point for the visibility and concern of education as an electoral issue. The increased focus on civil rights and additional amendments was one reason focus shifted to education at this time.

The rise of teachers' unions as a political influence also played a part. In 1960, the American Federation for Teachers (AFT) had a membership just greater than 50,000 teachers while the NEA had over 700,000; by 1978 that number had greatly increased and the AFT had greater than 500,000 members with just over 1.8 million members in the NEA (Smyth, 1980).

There was discussion about his support of a cabinet-level education position in the 1976 election as the reason Jimmy Carter was the first candidate to ever be endorsed by the National Education Association (Stallings, 2002; Smythe, 1980). Of the delegates at the 1976 Democratic National Convention, 180 were NEA members. "The NEA was acknowledged to be one of the key power bases of President Jimmy Carter . . . who repaid his debt by persuading Congress to establish a new Department of Education in 1979 (Ravitch, 1983; Elam, 1981). Then NEA executive director Terry Herndon acknowledged, "That's true. There'd be no department without the NEA" (Smyth, 1980).

Many thought this was a bad move. The *New York Times* ran an article in 1978, prior to the announcement of the department, saying, "The President is reported ready to propose creation of a Cabinet-level Department of Education. We hope the report is wrong; . . . it is an empty, even harmful idea, bad for the President, bad for the Cabinet, bad for education ("High price," 1978). Other interest groups such as the American Federation for Teachers (AFT), the Catholic Church, and conservatives were all opposed to the idea of a Department of Education and the cabinet-level position that would be associated with it (Elam, 1981).

The bill to create a Department of Education passed the House with a vote of 215 in favor and 201 opposed and the senate with a vote of 69 in favor and 22 opposed (Associated Press, 1979). The final rationale was that "elevating" education to full cabinet status would assure the nation's schools and colleges of greater federal attention and financial support. Decades later the need for the Department of Education was still in question (Education Week Library Staff, 2017a). Even after the vote, the department coalesced very slowly.

A DEPARTMENT OF EDUCATION

The Department of Education grew out of the humble beginnings of home education and an Office of Education within the Department of Health, Education, and Welfare. In the history of humans, schooling was initially a private matter, with each family and community providing information and teaching to the best of its ability and tailoring information to meet immediate needs. The first official school in the United States was the Boston Latin School founded in 1635. A historical document also records a "free school" in Virginia in 1635. At the time of the American Revolution, some cities and towns in the Northeast had free local schools paid for by all town residents (CEP, 2020).

The path from the first publicly supported schools to public education and Horace Mann set the stage for organized governmental units that oversee and direct federal funds toward education. This is an evolution from where the idea began with the Continental Congress. According to the George Washington University's Center on Education Policy, "The Founding Fathers maintained that the success of the fragile American democracy would depend on the competency of its citizens," and that "preserving democracy would require an educated population" (CEP, 2020).

There is much evidence that founding influencers Thomas Jefferson, John Adams, Samuel Adams, Benjamin Franklin, and even Noah Webster supported the idea of education for all; as it was never a constitutional right, school was allocated to the states and territories to add as they grew and could provide support. Jefferson stated in his 1786 letter to Georgy Wythe, "I think by far the most important bill in our whole code is that for the diffusion of knowledge among the people. No other sure foundation can be devised for the preservation of freedom, and happiness" (Jefferson, 1786).

Samuel Adams expressed the same idea some years earlier in a letter to James Warren when he wrote, "If Virtue & Knowledge are diffused among the People, they will never be enslaved. This will be their great Security" (Thorne, 2010). "Character and virtue were also considered essential to good citizenship, and education was seen as a means to provide moral instruction and build character" (CEP, 2020).

In the early years, this public support took the form of district support for aldermen and schoolhouses. As the years went on and towns grew, so did schools. The hope was that an educated public would create a meritocracy with each having the opportunity to demonstrate aptitude and ability. Federal ordinances passed in 1785 and 1787 gave acreage of federal lands to new states as they entered the union, with the agreement that a portion of this land be set aside for public schools.

The problem became that as schools were supported by local taxes, only wealthier areas were able to have well-furnished and supported schools. Children in rural, diverse, or impoverished neighborhoods were not getting the same access and accommodations that their counterparts in more affluent areas received. The 1800s saw the advent of Horace Mann who advocated for "common schools," which were to be free to all children, universally available, and funded by the state (CEP, 2020).

"Educating the poor and middle class would prepare them to obtain good jobs, proponents argued, and thereby strengthen the nation's economic position" (CEP, 2020). While not the sole reasons for education, advocates saw universal education as a means to eliminate poverty, crime, and other social problems. Some early leaders argued that the costs of properly educating children in public schools would be far less than the expenses of punishing and jailing criminals and coping with problems stemming from poverty (CEP, 2020).

"In 1830, about 55% of children aged 5 to 14 were enrolled in public schools; by 1870 this figure had risen to about 78%" (CEP, 2020). This was all positive, but even during this increase, many groups of nonwhite, immigrant, female, and non-Protestant students were discriminated against. Promoting equity for all became the mission of the public schools in the middle to late 1900s.

Brown v. Board of Education declared state-sponsored segregation of public schools to be unconstitutional and "public schools were placed in the vanguard of ensuring equity" (CEP, 2020). Many historians believe that the real beginning of educational politicization came during this time, with the passage of Title IV of the Civil Rights Act of 1964. Title IV was aimed at "guaranteeing an end to discrimination based on one's group identity." The Act represented "a clear affirmation of the equality of all persons before the law; explicitly barred the use of race, religion or national origin in school assignments or hiring practices" (Ravitch, 1983).

While Title VI focused on working with homelessness, it moved the federal government more solidly into a position of power as it maintains "no federal funds would go to any activity or program that practiced discrimination." As stated on the Department of Education website, "The anti-poverty and civil rights laws of the 1960s and 1970s brought about a dramatic emergence of the Department's equal access mission. The passage of laws such as Title VI of the Civil Rights Act of 1964, Title IX of the Education Amendments of 1972, and Section 504 of the Rehabilitation Act of 1973 which prohibited discrimination based on race, sex, and disability, respectively made civil rights enforcement a fundamental and long-lasting focus of the Department of Education" (U.S. Department of Education, 2021b).

When federal funds became tied to actions some thought the federal government had overstepped, while others thought the government finally had the ability to control what was happening in schools. Regardless, the result of funding being tied to actions has had a dramatic impact on education. The results of holding funds to influence school actions were seen in America 2000, No Child Left Behind, and Race to the Top, and now in the Biden administration's American Jobs and American Families Plans. There is no constitutional provision for complete federal support of education, so technically the states retain primary authority. Even with the increases in federal influence, the authority for U.S. education is distributed.

There are 50 state school systems plus the District of Columbia, Puerto Rico, and outlying territories. Within those state systems there are 13,598 regular school districts and 98,158 public schools.

State and local governments generally provide over 90% of the revenue available for public elementary and secondary education on an annual basis (CRS, 2019). Funds for public school revenue are only supported about 8% from the federal level.

Schools can receive basic grants, concentration grants, targeted grants, and education finance incentive grants. As an example, the ED Title I program directs grant funding toward schools with students from low-income families. During the 2015–2016 school year, nearly 56,000 public schools received Title I funds, reaching over 26 million students (Carlson, 2021). Remaining revenue for schools is generated from the state (47%) and local levels (45%) (CEP, 2020). The cost (adjusted for inflation) for education has increased from $7,785/student to $14,594/student and the list of things for which schools are responsible has grown exponentially (Volmer, 2021). Mandates are made by the federal government, with the costs being primarily covered by the states.

In addition to creating and overseeing the mandates created for the states, the Department of Education (ED) has other responsibilities. The department oversees and evaluates elementary and secondary schools. The department also has roles in enforcing civil rights. Finally, the department oversees postsecondary education and the distribution of student loans and grants.

The Secretary of Education

There are various opinions on what the role is for the secretary of education. In 1992, former Secretary Terrel Bell and his colleague at Terrel Bell and Associates, Donna L. Elmquist, published a review of Lamar Alexander's first year. Significant in this publication is the list of tasks described as the duties of the secretary of education. According to Bell and Elmquist, the secretary of education needs to do the following (1992):

- Lead American education by articulating its needs and rallying support from the president, cabinet, Congress, state and local lawmakers, and education leaders to address those needs.
- Administer the laws that Congress has enacted; see that all those who need to understand these laws interpret them accurately.
- Work closely with others to see that the federal role in education is faithfully executed in a manner most favorable to the nations' educational needs. The secretary should create new initiatives and program that will expand the federal role to meet newly emerging needs.
- Continually remind the president, cabinet, Congress, news media and the American public that education must be one of the highest priorities on the American agenda.
- Advocate educational research and improvement on a practical level. . . . The world is changing . . . and educational practices must keep pace
- The secretary should draw on the best minds from all industries to examine trends and issues in education and weigh alternatives to the status quo.
- The secretary should ensure that everyone in the nation enjoys the protection of the civil rights laws and access to equal opportunities.

This list is a description of the job of the secretary, from the viewpoint of someone who was a secretary. Additional descriptions from the U.S. Department of Education (U.S. Department of Education, 2010) describe the secretary as the person who leads the Department and promotes public understanding of the Department's mission, goals and objectives. The secretary is nominated by the president and confirmed by the Senate. As a member of the president's Cabinet, the secretary is the principal adviser to the president on federal policies, programs and activities related to education in the United States.

Another source indicates,

> The Secretary of Education has the job of helping to educate almost everyone—students, parents, migrant workers, Native Americans, and the handicapped. ... The Department funds bilingual teachers and minority language classes. The Secretary is responsible for four federally funded corporations—American Printing House for the Blind, Gallaudet University (for the deaf), Howard University (a predominantly black institution), the National Technical Institute for the Deaf & Rochester Institute of Technology (for the deaf) (Parker, 1978).

Officially, the U.S. Department of Education website says that "the Secretary is responsible for the overall direction, supervision, and coordination of all activities of the Department and is the principal adviser to the President on Federal policies, programs and activities related to education in the United States" (U.S. Department of Ed.ucation 2009). Regardless of which set of responsibilities are considered, the position of the secretary of education is influential not only to the Cabinet but to the millions of students who sit in class desks each school day. The ED operates the Office for Civil Rights, which protects students from discrimination or harassment in school (Carlton, 2021).

The secretary of education also oversees the management and distribution of the federal budget for education initiatives. Federal education funding goes to elementary and secondary school districts, postsecondary institutions, and college students. The largest part of the ED's budget goes to undergraduate and graduate students in the form of Pell Grants and federal student loans.

Fiscal year 2022 showed the Department of Education with $188.16 billion to allocate to its programs; this is quite an increase from where the department began (USA Spending, 2022). Forty-three years ago, in 1979 when the department was created, the budget was $14 billion (Langer, 2016). As the budget increased, it is worth examining how the responsibilities have changed.

There have been 12 official secretaries of education. The secretaries of education have been (in order of appearance):

1. Shirley M. Hufstedler
2. Terrel Bell
3. William J. Bennett

4. Lauro F. Cavazos, Jr.
5. Lamar Alexander
6. Richard Riley
7. Rod Paige
8. Margaret Spellings
9. Arne Duncan
10. John King, Jr.
11. Elizabeth "Betsy" DeVos
12. Miguel Cardona

In addition to appointed secretaries, there have been three men who have acted as secretary four times during vetting and waiting. Those who have served as acting secretaries of education are Ted Saunders, Phil Rosenthal, and Mitchell "Mick" Zais. This book will devote a chapter to each of the secretaries, as well as one chapter to the three acting secretaries. A short biography, the political context of each secretary's tenure, and the acts and bills they authorized will be discussed.

Chapter 1

Shirley M. Hufstedler
1979–1981

I am sure you will find, as I have, that a great many people are willing to fight over children, but precious few are willing to fight for them.... Your job, shorn of the paper and the bureaucracy, is to fight forcefully and joyfully for those kids.

—Shirley M. Hufstedler in a letter to Terrel Bell, 1981

Security is not the meaning of my life. Great opportunities are worth the risk.

—Shirley M. Hufstedler, Oral interviews, 2007

If you play it safe in life you've decided that you don't want to grow any more.

—Shirley M. Hufstedler, Oral interviews, 2007

The role of the teacher remains the highest calling of a free people. To the teacher, America entrusts her most precious resource, her children; and asks that they be prepared ... to face the rigors of individual participation in a democratic society.

—Shirley M. Hufstedler, Oral interviews, 2007

The highly quotable Shirly Mount Hufstedler was appointed the first secretary of education in 1979. At her nomination, she was described as "the small queenly woman who is smarter than almost everybody she talks to. She is [also] the senior woman judge in the land" (Smyth, 1980). A lawyer by trade, she had a passion for the underrepresented. "A bizarre creature," is what she called herself when she was first named as a Los Angeles superior court judge in 1961 (Levoy, 2016). Hufstedler was a direct and intelligent woman; she was also a trendsetter and used to being the first person to cross a threshold. She was "such an icon," said former federal prosecutor Andrea Ordin.

Shirley M. Hufstedler was born Shirly Ann Mount on August 24, 1925, in Denver, Colorado. Shirley's family moved frequently during her childhood. She attended 12 different schools between second and seventh grade. Her father was a contractor who moved all over the West bidding on public works projects. He left her mother when Shirley was six (Smyth, 1980). Her roots were a series of "very tough pioneer ladies." This may explain why she was willing to step up and take the position of education secretary, knowing it would be a challenge.

Shirley earned her bachelor's degree from the University of New Mexico. In 1949, Hufstedler was one of four women to enter her class at Stanford Law and one of two to graduate. Hufstedler, then Shirley Mount, was one of the cofounders of the *Stanford Law Review* and the only woman in its premier edition. While at Stanford, Shirley met and married Stan Hufstedler, who was the other cofounder of the *Law Review* (Ginsburg, 2017). She referred to her husband as "a non-stop genius" and her son said that "they really like each other . . . and he would like a relationship like that himself" (Smyth, 1980).

The Stanford Law School class of 1949, from which Shirley Mount graduated 10th, is known in California as "The Wonder Class" (Smyth, 1980). The graduates from that class went on to do great things. This included Hufstedler, despite a rocky start. Following law school, Hufstedler had a hard time finding employment. In her 2007 interview with the American History Channel (Hufstedler, 2007), she stated that no law firms were willing to hire her, even though she had solid reviews from her professors and alma mater.

Hufstedler opened a "one woman shop" and donated a half day a week to the Los Angeles Legal Aid Foundation. Her experience with the foundation was a substantial benefit to her legal career as it provided her quite a bit of time in court and in trials. She took cases other attorneys did not want and spent time ghost writing legal briefs for other lawyers (Hufstedler, 2007). It is also during this time that she gave birth to her only child, Steven (Hufstedler, 2007; Levoy, 2016).

Hufstedler was known by colleagues as "fierce" and a "lean writer" (Langer, 2016). "'She could say more with fewer words than any lawyer I have ever practiced with,' said her colleague, Mark McDonald" (Levoy, 2016). Colleagues described her as a "civil libertarian and a feminist sensitive to the concerns of the minorities." She maintained close relationships with these colleagues and their families and was a valued mentor. Hufstedler helped younger women who were trying to break into the law profession.

Her ability to do solid work helped her gain recognition, and in 1960 she was appointed special legal consultant to the attorney general of California in the Colorado River litigation. Hufstedler began her judicial career when she was named to the Los Angeles Superior Court in 1961, holding this position as the only woman among the court's 120 judges. Her first task was to create the "written tentative opinion" along with other administrative improvements. Five years later, she was appointed associate justice of the California Court of Appeal (Hufstedler, 2007).

While the creation of the "written tentative opinion" does not sound like much, it is an example of the type of efficiency and directness that the public could expect from Hufstedler. The new format of opinion created by Hufstedler shared the judge's opinion on a case and helped guide further argument, directing argument away from issues that were not germane to the matter at hand. "Los Angeles Superior Court's law and motion department continues to issue tentative rulings today" (Konick, 2014). Hufstedler approached creating the Department of Education the same way—she directed solutions toward what she believed was most important.

"The Superior Court proved just a quick stop on a professional tour that would take her to the 9th Circuit Court of Appeals, and then to the U.S. Department of Education as the agency's first leader" (Levoy, 2016). Hufstedler was appointed to the U.S. Court of Appeals for the Ninth Circuit by President Lyndon B. Johnson in 1968. She was only the second woman on a federal circuit court, as well as being the only woman for 11 years as a federal appellate judge. Personal interviews with Hufstedler indicate that she believed Lady Bird Johnson, the first lady, was responsible for her appointment.

Hufstedler was "the favorite to be nominated to the Supreme Court during the Carter administration if a seat arose" (Langer, 2016). Instead of a Supreme Court seat, in 1979 Hufstedler was named to a new cabinet post as secretary of education by President Carter, with support from Los Angeles mayor Tom Bradley and Senator Alan Cranston. Secretary Hufstedler has been recorded saying more than once that she knew she was on the short list for those to be considered as secretary of education by President Carter, but she had no idea she was "the whole list" (Hufstedler, 2007). A Carter administration official at the time was quoted as saying that her liberal rulings over the years on civil rights cases had helped gain her the post (Levoy, 2016).

Hufstedler dealt with education issues while on the bench and had firm opinions about the importance of education (Ujifusa, 2016). "During her eleven years as a judge on the U.S. Court of Appeals for the 9th Circuit, an opinion on which she wrote and was particularly proud of was a dissent in *Lau v. Nichols*." *Lau v. Nichols* was a case that involved the San Francisco School District's failure to provide English-language instruction to around

1,800 children of Chinese ancestry. "[B]y the time [I] became Secretary of Education, we then had in place the so-called Lau Regulations, which was a reflection of that decision and about equal protection for youngsters whose initial language was not English," Hufstedler said in the interview. "So I thought that was an achievement that I've always enjoyed a lot."

The Senate approved Hufstedler on November 30, 1979, in an 81 to 2 vote. When asked why she took the position, she responded that "when your President asks you to do something, you do it." She was given a $14 billion budget (Langer, 2016). Hufstedler served the newly created Department of Education from 1979 until 1981. As the department's first secretary, her chief responsibilities were helping to shift education policy work from what was then the Department of Health, Education and Welfare to the new stand-alone cabinet-level education department (Ujifusa, 2016).

Hufstedler worked to create a cohesive department where one had never existed. "She was serious about bringing people together and having them work in a serious way," said her chief of staff, Marshall "Mike" Smith (Ujifusa, 2016). As education secretary, Hufstedler oversaw the creation of a new department of the federal government, a process fraught with bureaucratic complexity.

The new agency absorbed more than 150 government education programs previously administered by five departments, although principally the Department of Health, Education, and Welfare, which in the realignment became the Department of Health and Human Services. Hufstedler was able to open the doors of the ED a month ahead of schedule and $9 million below budget (Hufstedler, 1981). One of the first things Hufstedler had to do when she took office was finalize her budget.

Per the 1974 Budget Act, the president presents his budget to Congress in late January/early February. Carter gave her 90 days to get the department to a functioning level, which she achieved within only 60 days, using half of the allotted budget (Ginsburg, 2017). New to the position and department and sworn in in late November, Hufstedler had to do in days what other departments had been doing since the prior year. When she agreed to accept the position, she confirmed that she could learn to create a budget and worked closely with the Office of Management and Budget (Hufstedler, 2007).

Hufstedler's advice to the incoming secretary as she left included this warning: "The first thing you must tackle—and I mean literally the first—will be your departmental budget. My hand was barely off the swearing-in Bible before it was on the budget book. I was informed the President would expect my budget appeals immediately—preferably by the time I got back to my office" (Hufstedler, 1981). She also cautioned that nothing would "make or break your reputation and effectiveness" in Washington than the "speed and detail" with which he handled the budget.

In a 2007 interview, she reflected that her position as secretary was a "horrendously difficult job" and there was not a great deal of enthusiasm about a woman, about a Department of Education, or about civil rights. Shirley Hufstedler was a champion of the rights of women and minorities. She supported Title I programs for needy students and backed funding increases for women's athletic programs. "Bigotry," she remarked, "has always been much more popular than one likes to believe" (Langer, 2016).

Hufstedler sought to assuage fears about the office and her mission and presented a vision of the new agency as a guarantor of educational equity. There was a great deal of tension during those years. Among the most controversial issues of the time was busing. As secretary, Hufstedler argued that "surely busing youngsters for the purpose of achieving racial integration is not a first resort." But there were many situations, she said, "in which it must not be the last resort" (Langer, 2016).

Hufstedler remembers working 18 to 20 hours a day. Unfortunately, in addition to having a new position and department, Hufstedler came to Washington in the middle of a hiring freeze. Regardless of the freeze, she was committed to a diverse workforce (Hufstedler, 2007). She hired accordingly when she could.

Hufstedler saw the national impact of education on the nation's security. She cited that "fewer and fewer of our students are learning the rudiments of math and science" and U.S. students were being outpaced by Germany, Japan, and Russia. Hufstedler also saw a national interest in upgrading language capabilities. "Our schools may be the worst in the industrialized world at teaching languages other than English." At that time, she said the Soviet Union had 10 million students taking English (Hufstedler, 1981).

Hufstedler took office at a tumultuous time in U.S. history. During Carter's presidency there was much focus on energy, the Middle East, and the Soviets. The summer before Congress approved the Department of Education, Carter signed the Strategic Arms Limitation Treaty (SALT) with Russia. In 1979, just prior to when Hufstedler was sworn, the Iran hostage crisis began when 52 Americans were taken by Iranian revolutionaries and held for 444 days.

In 1980 many things happened, from a grain embargo on Russia to boycotting the 1980 Olympics which were held in Moscow. A full recession was called in April 1980 and in November of that year Carter lost reelection. Ronald Reagan was elected president. All these factors influenced Hufstedler's tenure—from impacting the cost of fuel oil needed to heat schools and run buses to the influx of refugees that the Department of Education now handled that did not speak English (Hufstedler, 1981).

Americans were at the height of the cold war. Competition with Russia was fierce, and while education was seen as a way through that, the rise of unions that impacted education policy may have looked too much like

Soviet workers' unions to be embraced by politicians and the general public. Opponents of the Education Department feared federal intrusion in local schools and undue influence of these teachers' unions.

Hufstedler sought to assuage those fears and presented a vision of the new agency as a guarantor of educational equity. "When we think about what we're about and the programs we are going to try to keep," the *New York Times* quoted her telling her staff, "we ought to think about who is the most vulnerable. The most seriously disadvantaged must be protected first" (Langer, 2016). Secretary Hufstedler accomplished the goal set out for her by the NEA and President Carter. "Hufstedler's success in her dual effort to form the Department out of nothing and to introduce the idea of a national agenda for education established a platform on which her successors could build to keep the Department alive (Stallings, 2002).

Hufstedler also set goals to streamline and strengthen the political workings of the federal–state relationship, reinforce the notion that the department would not supersede local control by attempting to impose restrictive regulations, focus on educational equity, and finally, make education important to the nation again "to elevate the consciousness of Americans about the good work classroom teachers do" (Stallings, 2002).

As Hufstedler prepared to vacate the office, it was not lost on her or anyone else that whoever came next would need to help the president decide if the department she had worked tirelessly to create should be disassembled or remain intact. Her advice to incoming Secretary Bell was outlined in "Open Letter to a Cabinet Member" (Hufstedler, 1981); it contained much advice but also highlighted the biggest obstacle Bell would encounter, "you will face one obstacle which I did not. You will need to convince your President that your department . . . is necessary."

Hufstedler told Bell that his "prestige and authority as a Cabinet Secretary will greatly ease the progress of important education legislation through the congress." She recommended how he watches various bills and moves things forward. She closed with "I hope you will use these opportunities to teach America about our schools, as well as to articulate important national problems in education. You can do much to put the needs of America's children on the front pages where they belong" (Hufstedler, 1981). It turns out that with Bell's prior experience in DC under his belt, she need not have worried. Hufstedler passed away March 30, 2016, at the age of 90.

Chapter 2

Terrel Bell
1981–1985

There are three things to emphasize in teaching: The first is motivation, the second is motivation, and the third is (you guessed it) motivation.

—Terrel Bell

One of the highest priorities in all my years in education has been to provide leadership in building a truly great teaching profession.

—Terrel Bell, *The Thirteenth Man*, 1988

All, regardless of race or class or economic status, are entitled to a fair change and to the tools for developing their individual powers of mind and spirit to the utmost. This promise means that all children by virtue of their own efforts, competently guided, can hope to attain the mature and informed judgment needed to secure gainful employment, and to manage their own lives, thereby serving not only their own interests but also the progress of society itself.

—*A Nation at Risk*, 1983

At the time Terrel Bell was asked to be secretary of education, he had already spent substantial time in Washington, DC, serving education and his country. Secretary of education was not the first position Bell had at the national level. While national education was under the Department of Health, Education, and Welfare, Terrel Bell was U.S. commissioner of education under both President Nixon and President Ford (1988).

The road to secretary of education from the path on which he began is impressive. Terrel Bell was born in 1921 in a small town in Idaho and grew up in poverty. One of nine children raised by a widow, he lived in a one-room house with no indoor plumbing. Bell graduated from high school and continued to Albion State Normal school. Halfway through his college career, Terrel Bell registered for the marines in response to the Japanese bombing of Pearl Harbor.

Bell credits his time in the military for helping him learn to keep his opinions to himself. He tells the story of offering suggestions to his basic training instructors about how they could improve what they were doing, which earned him 72 hours in solitary confinement. After the marines, Bell stayed in education. He finished his bachelor's degree, got a master's degree from the University of Idaho, and then a doctorate from the University of Utah (Sweeney, 1981).

Bell emphasized freedom of speech and "freedom from speech" (Sweeney, 1981). Interestingly, one of the things that gained Bell recognition is the idea that children should not be required to participate in things they and their families find offensive. If there were assignments or material that could be found offensive, Bell believed that students should have options for alternate materials.

Bell outlined the reasoning on this issue as follows: for students, so many things are required. Attendance is required. Passing classes is required; if reading something hurtful or disturbing puts students in a position of having to choose between reading the offensive material or not passing, that is not fair. Bell believed a "police state" should not make children read things that were offensive or that were against their family beliefs.

While Bell did not support book burning or pulling books off library shelves, he did believe that the required reading curriculum should be something that was palatable, hopeful, and uplifting for all children. He believed children should not have to read authors like J. D. Salinger and Chaucer as part of their curriculum but should be offered options. He thought that offering "offensive books" as an alternative curriculum was fine, but requiring them of kids who had no option was not fair.

In addition to advocating that students have more control over their curriculum, Bell is known for his support of bilingual education for all students, stating that students should not be monolingual (UPI Archives, 1982). As commissioner, Bell approved the bilingual guidelines that have encouraged hundreds of school systems to start bilingual programs for children who have little or no command of English. This support of bilingual education programs continued during his time as secretary. Bell's support for students who may struggle is also evident in his support of equality in education and his belief in the department's mission "to advocate, monitor and support equal educational opportunity" (Bell, 1988).

Bell was also very supportive of teachers. "One of the highest priorities during all my years in education has been to provide leadership in building a truly great teaching profession." As today, in 1981 the teaching profession was in trouble. "Morale was terrible. Salaries were dreadfully low. Respect for teachers was commensurate with their salaries" (Bell, 1988). Bell would say that our schools' performance deficiencies could be traced directly to the "pitiful" standing of teachers in American society.

Bell supported a merit pay scale, with the idea of rewarding teachers who were doing an exceptional job. While the plan failed in Utah, he continued to support merit pay. This support of teachers, parents, high quality education for all students, and in particular those who did not have access, were characteristics that he highlighted as superintendent in Utah. These ideals also put him in the running when selection was under way for the second secretary of education.

When Ronald Reagan ran for office, he promised his voters he would abolish the Department of Education (Bell, 1988). There was speculation that Reagan would not fill the cabinet-level position but would let it die. Bell was recommended to Reagan by Casper Weinberger, who had worked with Commissioner Bell while secretary of health, education, and welfare. Ed Meese, who was counselor to the president from 1981 to 1985, was the first person to have a formal discussion with Bell regarding appointment to the secretary position.

Meese and Bell met in San Diego and following that meeting, Bell was certain he did not want to be secretary and that the Reagan team did not want him (Bell, 1988). Four days after the meeting in San Diego, Bell was called to Washington, DC, to meet with Reagan. Reagan was clear that he believed education was a state-level concern and had, as did his advisors, fear of federal control.

Reagan asked Bell to draft alternatives to then current policies and made it clear he did not want rubber stamps, "Let's hear about the issues. I don't need yes men" (Bell, 1988). Reagan eventually asked Bell to be secretary of education. Bell conferred with his wife and took the position. Terrel Bell was sworn in as the second secretary of education in January 1981. Bell was not a yes man.

When Bell took office, he was "threatened" with overseeing the abolition of the department (Dodge, 2002) and was actually tasked with disbanding it. Bell knew what he was up against. Although he had testified for Carter in support of a department (Bell, 1988), Bell took the job because he thought he could change Reagan's mind. Bell was a self-proclaimed zealot who had "been involved in the war against ignorance and neglect for thirty-five years" (Bell, 1988).

Bell supported a federal-level agency that was not "a captive of HEW." The U.S. Department of Education was created from units that were part of the former Department of Health, Education, and Welfare (HEW). It had a budget of $14.7 billion and over 7,000 employees (Bell, 1988). In January 1981, the department had only really been in existence since May 1980. Bell faced opposition and political tension from the time he began office.

From Bell's initial meeting with Ed Meese in San Diego, it was evident that a solid faction of the Reagan team: Anderson, Meese, and James, as well as Reagan, believed that education should be a lower-level agency (Bell, 1988). Bell took office in January and by late February/early March 1981 he was being nudged to close the department. In political movements, some of the nudging took form in the repeated blocking of candidates Bell was submitting to be appointed to the department. To demonstrate his political prowess and undermine those who were subverting him, Bell hatched a plan.

As previously stated, Bell was a proponent of bilingual education, but regulations to bilingual education proposed by Hufstedler were, in Bell's words, "dead wrong" (Bell, 1988). Bell withdrew Hufstedler's regulations, gaining him the trust of those who opposed the department. Once the regulations were subdued, Bell and the administration felt the backlash: educators and Hispanic leaders were upset. These leaders called, wrote, and visited their representatives. This was all part of Bell's plan.

Bell demonstrated his educational understanding, diplomacy, and support of the president. A proposal for English as a Second Language (ESL) curricula replaced the bilingual regulations as a superior alternative and Reagan saw the benefit and impact Bell could have (Bell, 1988). This point/counterpoint—proposing one program to substitute for another—became the type of political back and forth that peppered Bell's tenure in the ED.

This political back and forth did not subside until then director of the National Institute of Education, Ed Curran, made recommendations without Bell's knowledge. Curran was a presidential appointment and Bell immediately called for Curran's resignation. Bell stepped in and asked for support from the president and requested Curran be removed. Curran was removed from his office and transferred to a different department and Bell did not have problems with his adversaries again.

The credit for keeping the department alive during Reagan's first term is held by Bell (Stallings, 2002). Bell convinced the president and Congress not to split the department into several departments by convincing them that all the laws the Department of Education oversaw required coordination. Bell also explained that ensuring grant approval and funds allocations were accredited and complied with the law was more easily coordinated by one office (Bell, 1988).

The importance and usefulness of a federal role in education became clearer and the president grew more amenable to the idea of preserving the Department of Education (Stallings, 2002). Whatever Bell was doing, it was working—in Washington and in the press. On July 27, 1982, *U.S. News and World Report* ranked Bell as the fifth most effective cabinet member (Bell, 1988).

The role of the Department of Education changed during the Reagan years and, as with other Reagan era policies, much of the focus was to "return things to the original intent of the Founding Fathers," which in educational terms meant more local control with the role of the department moving back to a data collection tool (Stallings, 2002). Bell managed to accomplish many of Reagan's goals without dismantling the department.

The major impacts Bell had in the department, and certainly those that have had the longest impact, were first and foremost, keeping the department together, advancing the movement toward need-based loan programs, and creating the National Commission on Excellence in Education. Bell called attention to the state of American schools when he created the national commission and released *A Nation at Risk* in 1983 (Dodge, 2002).

A NATION AT RISK

In 1983 education reform entered a new era (Adams, n.d.). There was a belief that the deterioration of the American economy was caused by a lack of international competitiveness because of the inadequately trained labor force. This lack of training was especially true in the South, which trailed the nation in school expenditures as well as student achievement (Vinovskis, 1999).

President Reagan established an 18-member blue ribbon panel in August 1981 to determine how effective the nation's schools were (Mirga, 1982). The president commissioned Secretary Bell to convene the committee. The committee was chaired by then president of the University of Utah, David P. Gardner (Adams, n.d.), and was called the National Committee on Excellence in Education (NCEE). The committee held hearings for 18 months that collected information from experts and ordinary citizens (Bell, 1988). The NCEE produced *A Nation at Risk,* a report which was presented to Bell and the American people in April 1983 (NCEE, 1983).

The report states that the committee was charged with six specific tasks:
- assess the quality of teaching and learning in our Nation's public and private schools, colleges, and universities;

- compare American schools and colleges with those of other advanced nations;
- study the relationship between college admissions requirements and student achievement in college;
- identify educational programs which result in notable student success in college;
- assess the degree to which major social and educational changes in the last quarter century have affected student achievement; and
- define problems which must be faced and overcome if we are to successfully pursue the course of excellence in education. (NCEE, 1983)

An interim report supported the expected results that U.S. students are falling behind. There were two unexpected midpoint findings: (1) the commission found fault with the textbook publishing industry, stating that the publishers underestimate the students, and (2) they feared the creation of haves and have-nots based on access to microcomputers (Mirga, 1982). The final results of the report moved education reform into a time when federal measurement and input became common.

"The excellence era" in education reform was launched, ushering in more than two decades of federal, state, and local initiatives to improve America's public schools (Adams, n.d.). The report found that American students compared poorly relative to students overseas, high levels of U.S. adults were functionally illiterate, and achievement test scores were declining (Adams, n.d.).

As evidence for this, NCEE noted that the increased enrollment in college remedial courses, increased workforce expenditures on remedial education, low expectations for students, less time devoted to instruction and homework, and poor teacher preparation and pay (NCEE, 1983; Adams, n.d.). The list for how to address the recommendations was lengthy. Recommendations included tougher high school graduation requirements, more rigorous and measurable standards of student performance, increased instructional time, improved teaching and teaching preparation, increased fiscal support and better school leadership (Adams, n.d.).

As could be expected, there was a lot of excitement about these results. Following the report, many educators warned the public not to be alarmed. "The conditions described in that report, while evident to some degree in some schools, are not universal" (Vik, 1984). It was speculated that this report had so much impact because it came during a time of great change and "against a backdrop of widespread concern regarding the health of the U.S. economy" (Adams, n.d.).

Although President Reagan's popularity was high, the nation itself had not been in great shape since 1981: inflation was in the double digits and unemployment was widespread. America's prestige and influence had declined and the taking of the hostages in Tehran left many feeling angry and impotent (Bell, 1988). *A Nation at Risk* reflected contemporary misgivings that America was losing its once unchallenged preeminence in commerce and technology (Adams, n.d.). The general malaise of the public was reflected in the schools (Bell, 1988). In response to this malaise, schools and colleges also became a scapegoat for the problems that were being seen in the country.

The NCEE report was supposed to rally the American people around the schools and colleges (Bell, 1988). It was the hope of the committee that when the report was released, just as was the case after the 1957 launch of Sputnik, the comparison between U.S. and foreign schools would elicit an increase in funding to local schools from the federal government (Vik, 1984). While there is no direct proof that increased funding was tied directly to *A Nation at Risk*, there is causal data that indicates that from the 1980s to the 1990s the cost for education per student (adjusted for inflation) rose approximately $1,500 per student (Vollmer, 2021).

THE WORLD DURING BELL'S TIME AS SECRETARY

During Bell's time as secretary, the national and international stage were rife with political issues. This was the height of the cold war. The years from 1981 to 1985 were filled with discovery, innovation, and change. Some of these issues were positive: in 1981, Sandra Day O'Connor was the first woman appointed to the Supreme Court (education side note: many thought it should have been Shirley Hufstedler, see Chapter 2), the Iran hostages were released, and the Vietnam Memorial was erected in 1982.

Also in 1982, the first successful artificial heart transplant was completed. In 1983, Sally K. Ride became the first U.S. woman astronaut to be sent into space. The 1984 Olympics were held in Los Angeles, California, and Mary Lou Retton won two gold medals. In 1985, the U.S. Balanced Budget Bill was enacted.

Some of the issues that occurred between 1981 and 1985 were negative. In 1981, the nation saw the first reported case of the AIDS (acquired immune deficiency syndrome) virus. There was an assassination attempt and President Reagan was shot.

The Equal Rights Amendment died three state votes short of ratification. Mexico's economy collapsed. The embassy in Beirut was bombed. Hackers invaded the Los Alamos Laboratory and the U.S. invaded Grenada. Indira Gandhi was shot. The Soviets boycotted the Olympics in Los Angeles. The first hole in the ozone, detected in 1977, was verified. Ethiopia blocked the airlift of Ethiopian Jews. Crack cocaine appeared on the national scene.

Other issues, depending on your viewpoint, may have been neutral. Apple introduced the first MacIntosh computer in 1984. MTV aired in August 1981. Prince Charles married Lady Di and Reagan stopped an air traffic controller strike. Pac Man debuted in 1981. Liposuction was introduced. Reagan introduced the Star Wars program as a national defense agenda. Camcorders and Cabbage Patch Kids were introduced.

Ronald Reagan was reelected. Stonewashed jeans became fashionable. Run D.M.C. had the first rap gold album. "We Are the World" was recorded to raise aid for Africa. Gorbachev was elected the last president of Russia. An extra second was added to the world calendar. Nintendo and New Coke were introduced. During this time, the population of the U.S increased by 6 million people: from 231,665,458 in 1981 to 237,923,795 in 1985. Federal spending and debt followed a similar trajectory, with the federal debt in 1985 being $1817.5 billion. (Infoplease, 2017). Cable News Network (CNN) emerged and so did the 24-hour news cycle.

There was a lot of change during these years, and with the rise of technology people were more aware, in close to real time, of issues than they had been in previous decades. This feel of change and momentum may have impacted the motion in the Oval Office and in the cabinet departments. After battling those who opposed the department for so long, Bell resigned in November 1984 with the department intact.

Chapter 3

William J. Bennett
1985–1988

If there is one thing educators can agree on, it's this: children do better in school when their parents get involved in their learning.

—William J. Bennett

The elementary school must assume as its sublime and most solemn responsibility the task of teaching every child in it to read. Any school that does not accomplish this has failed.

—William J. Bennett

Get kids with the right teachers and we can educate them.

—William J. Bennett

If Bell was brought in because he was a known quantity, diplomatic and safe, Dr. William J. Bennett was brought in because he was the opposite. Bennett brought notoriety to the department and was quite controversial due to his conservative morals-based ideals. *Time* magazine ran an article in May 1985 titled "Education: The Secretary of Controversy: William Bennett. "Bell's administration may have secured the continued existence of the department, but William Bennett, Reagan's next appointee, secured its fame (Stallings, 2002).

William John Bennett was born July 3, 1943, in Brooklyn, New York. His family later moved to Washington, DC. Young Bill graduated from the Gonzaga College High School, which is a Catholic boys school. Bennett went to college to play football and graduated from Williams College with a bachelor's degree in philosophy. He received a PhD in political philosophy from the University of Texas in 1970 and a law degree from Harvard in 1971.

Bennett worked his way through college and graduate school, but still graduated with $12,000 in student loans (Encyclopedia.com, 2018a). Bennett credits these formative years with creating an understanding and appreciation of role models, "heroes," for moral development and for teaching him to speak his mind, "We were taught at home to speak our minds. You had to speak your mind or you wouldn't get a chance to talk" (Gross, 2012).

Initially registered as a Democrat, Bennett changed his registration to Republican. Bennett worked in higher education as an associate professor, an associate dean, and an assistant to the president, all the while, writing and increasing his notoriety. In 1976, Bennett became the executive director of the National Humanities Center, which he cofounded with Charles Frankel. In 1979, intruders murdered Frankel, and Bennett assumed his office as president (Encyclopedia.com, 2018a).

In 1981, President Ronald Reagan appointed Bennett as director of the National Endowment for the Humanities. Bennett joked that he "was a professor of the humanities and one of three humanities professors who voted for Reagan at the time. I was the second one he asked and the first to say yes" (Gross, 2012). As director he was "abrasive and controversial." Bennett had strong ideas about the humanities. Bennett wanted to work toward a definition of the humanities that was more aligned with Western values (Encyclopedia.com, 2018a).

In February 1985, William J. Bennett became the third secretary of education. Reagan brought Bennett in because "he did not think he could get rid of that department, so instead wanted Bennett to represent the views of the American people, *not* specific interest groups." Bennett agreed (Bennett, 1988). For conservatives, the department was "generally viewed as a disaster." From the Democrats, the department was viewed as a conduit to money.

The Department of Education had been created as a "political deal" between President Carter and the National Education Association and, as a result, conservatives believed the department would serve special interests. Bennett believed that it was necessary to keep interest groups out and in all of this, the president was his key person (Bennett, 1988). Bennett looked to Reagan's policies and political ideals to direct how he approached his appointment as secretary.

A month in as secretary, Bennett announced, "I have more affinity with the views of the American people than do most of my academic colleagues. I think I am in the mainstream of American thinking (Bowen, 1985). In Bennett's first press conference, he supported Reagan's budget cuts in the student loan program (Encyclopedia.com, 2018a): a $2.3 billion cut (Bowen, 1985), which was not popular with many. Bennett categorized federal financial aid as a "boondoggle" for affluent families. In Bennett's opinion, it was unfair to tax people who had saved for and paid tuition in order to cover the financial aid of students whose families had not done the same.

Bennett was not only vocal about the cuts to the student loan program, but also supported vouchers for the parents of elementary and secondary education students who were dissatisfied with their children's school experience. In general, he opposed major federal education programs. There were those who were opposed to Bennett's ideals. "Many people were disturbed at the Administration's efforts to reverse the Government's long-term commitment to federal help for education. 'If you are not a supporter of a federal role,' said . . . [the] president of the American Council on Education, 'you should not be in that job'" (Bowen, 1985).

In an interview about the Reagan years, Bennett identified his priorities as secretary:

1. Improve American Education by focusing on curriculum
2. Focus on bilingual education by making sure that kids became fluent in English
3. Give parents choice in the education of their children
4. Tie teacher compensation with performance
5. Focus on value education (Bennett, 1988)

Bennett came to the department with the goals of a reorganization of the department and the elimination of the National Institute of Education (which was the research branch of the U.S. Department of Education). He was interested in changing how student loans were distributed to reduce the total student aid budget and wanted to reintroduce a core curriculum rooted in Western thought. He wanted the curriculum to pay attention to the three Cs: content, character, and choice (Education Week Library Staff, 2017e).

Bennett believed that his job was to keep the debate on education going and that he was to represent at the federal level the views of the American people. Bennett felt the need to take up the public fight and part of that was fighting special interest groups. From 1963 to 1978, just prior to the release of *A Nation at Risk*, the U.S. saw the worst education decline it had ever seen (Bennett, 1988). Bennett wanted to make sure this decline did not get swept under the carpet.

Bennett believed that special interest groups were responsible for student achievement, because they had been in control. Bennett continued to have choice words about the National Education Association and their practices. Bennett claimed that the NEA leadership "has long since lost any legitimacy to speak on behalf of the field of American education" (Olson, 1987).

In turn, the president of the National Education Association, Mary Hatwood Futrell, fired back. Ms. Futrell asserted that—when compared with its "rhetoric about excellence in education"—the Reagan administration's proposed education budget was "nothing short of duplicitous." The bottom-line consideration was the federal role in education (Olson, 1987).

During his first six weeks in office, Bennett focused on personnel and fired many of those who had been employed within the department. He needed and created a public affairs office. Bennett and his colleagues believed that the "real work" in education was done at the state and local level. Historically, the flow of information from the federal agency to the states was done through special interest groups. Bennett knew that he and his staff needed to deliver the message directly so that there was no misrepresentation. When his staff was in order, Bennett found time to get on the road.

Bennett gained a reputation as a secretary who was committed to improving children's education by seeing what was going on firsthand by visiting over 150 schools (Dodge, 2002). Bennett "crisscrossed the country to deliver speeches, teach sample lessons, critique higher education and espouse the value of rooting curriculum in traditional Western thought." He credits his wife, an elementary and special education teacher, with this approach (Gross, 2012). When Bennett took the position as secretary, she told him he needed to "do his homework," go to school, talk to teachers, and teach classes. This approach gained Bennett credibility, even for those with whom he disagreed.

In May 1986, Education Secretary William J. Bennett formed the National Assessment Governing Board (NAGB). This 21-member group was referred to as the Alexander-James study group (because it was headed by Gov. Lamar Alexander and H. Thomas James) (Shaw, 1986). The purpose of the NAGB was to review the National Assessment of Educational Progress (NAEP).

The NAEP is the largest nationally representative, continuing evaluation of education in the United States. This assessment served as a national yardstick of student achievement since 1969 (NAGB, 2020). The Alexander-James study group reviewed the NAEP and, while in general, praised elementary schools, but criticized the lack of state-level information and excessive regulation of the principalship (Shaw, 1986; Vinoviskas, 1999). The lack of state-level information resulted, in part, as the reauthorization of the Elementary and Secondary Education Act of 1965 (ESEA). While it was a goal of Bennett to make budgetary cuts while he was there, the Education Department budget actually grew.

During Bennett's tenure, the department released documents with department goals and information. A reauthorization of the 1965 ESEA moved toward academic achievement and away from mere regulation compliance (Stallings, 2002). Bennett was the coauthor of *First Lessons: A Report on Elementary Education,* published by the U.S. Office of Education in 1987.

First Lessons lists his personal convictions concerning elementary education (Encyclopedia.com, 2018b). In addition, Bennett wrote

- *James Madison High School: A Curriculum for American Students* (December 1987, as secretary of the Department of Education)
- *James Madison Elementary School: A Curriculum for American Students* (August 1988, as secretary of the Department of Education)

These books, along with future books by Bennett, focused on a classical education, American history, increased family values, and family involvement in a child's education.

IN THE NEWS DURING THIS TIME

The years 1985–1988 continued the trend of major changes on both national and global fronts. These three years were busy—in popular and political cultures. New Coke came out, crack cocaine appeared, the wreck of the *Titanic* was found and explored by a robotic arm, and "We Are the World" was recorded. Daniel Ortega became president of Nicaragua. Hezbollah was founded. The Russians conducted nuclear arms tests. Reagan and Gorbachev met for the first time in Geneva, and Kasparov became the youngest world chess champion. ("What Happened in 1985–1988," 2014).

The Iran-Contra affair was under way. Martin Luther King Jr. Day was established. Aruba became independent, there was a revolution in the Philippines, and Spain and Portugal became part of the European community. The Ugandan government was overthrown. The Chernobyl nuclear disaster occurred. FOX television began. The Unabomber appeared on the scene. The Simpsons premiered on television. The Summer Olympics were held in Seoul, Korea. In addition, there was a high number of plane crashes and natural disasters.

Bennett resigned from the department in 1988 to take a place in the law firm of Dunnels, Duvall, Bennett, and Porter. Despite the department's request for a lower budget while he was there, the budget of the Department of Education actually increased (Bennett, 1988). Bennett believed that his greatest accomplishment as secretary of education was that he and his department did what they said they would: they kept the debate about education going and moved it to the forefront.

Of his work at the department, Bennett most enjoyed visiting schools and being a substitute teacher (Bennett, 1988). He enjoyed teaching and working with students and teachers. Bennett supported many things: increased training for teachers, increased involvement for families, and the deregulation of the principalship. Bennett raised awareness about the quality of education being paid for by U.S. tax dollars from kindergarten through the university level and questioned, what he believed to be, the exploitative nature of federal student financial aid.

As a result of these issues and a perceived lack of willingness to address them, Bennett called Congress his "biggest disappointment" (Bennett, 1988; Rothman, 1988) and the secretary position the greatest job he ever had. His advice to the future secretary was to "like to go to schools" and to believe that "the possibility of the job is real. You can provide a constructive contribution."

Chapter 4

Lauro F. Cavazos, Jr.
1988–1990

We must do better or perish as the nation we know today.

—Lauro F. Cavazos, Jr.

In 1988, Lauro F. Cavazos, Jr., was sworn in as the fourth secretary of education. Cavazos was quiet and a 180-degree departure from Bill Bennett. Critics believed that Reagan was putting a secretary in place that would support Bush's identity as the education president (Stallings, 2002), a role that both he and the first lady supported. Cavazos served under both Presidents Reagan and Bush.

Lauro Cavazos was born in 1927 on a large ranch outside of Kingsville, Texas. He was a sixth generation Texan with Mexican heritage. A product of the public schools, Cavazos attended until he enlisted and served in World War II. He returned from the war and earned bachelor's and master's degrees in zoology from Texas Tech. Lauro received a PhD in physiology from the University of Iowa in 1954. Cavazos taught anatomy and later became a university president at Texas Tech. Cavazos married, and he and his wife went on to have ten children.

Lauro Cavazos was appointed as the secretary of education by Ronald Reagan on September 20, 1988. Cavazos was the first person of Hispanic descent appointed to a cabinet position. As a result of his appointment, Lauro Cavazos was awarded the National Hispanic Leadership Award from the League of United Latin American Citizens (Encyclopedia.com, 2019). The Reagan appointment of Cavazos to secretary of education was seen by many as a move to secure the Hispanic presidential vote for then Vice President George H. W. Bush. Reagan and Cavazos both denied this allegation stating that Cavazos was a qualified appointment and had been considered in 1981.

Cavazos was respected by the education community for his knowledge of curriculum and his understanding of Hispanic students. He vowed to seek better funding for schools, focus federal services on high-risk children, and improve outcomes, especially for Hispanic, Indigenous, and immigrant students. In his two years as education secretary, Cavazos was known for promoting the idea of giving parents the option of deciding where to send their children to school (with limits to prevent segregation) and advocating for bilingual education (Associated Press, 2022).

Cavazos had three major goals for his term as secretary of education. The first goal was to generate public support for the national goals adopted by the president and governors after the 1989 National Governors Association (NGA) National Education Summit. The second goal was to encourage school choice and participation for parents. Cavazos's third goal was to defend student loans.

In September 1989, President George H. W. Bush had called together the nation's governors to discuss the future of national education and education reform. Given the strong belief within both the Reagan and Bush administrations that education historically has been and should be primarily a local and state responsibility, it made sense for the federal government to work closely with the NGA to reform American schooling.

Based upon the deliberations there, six national education goals were developed. They were first announced by President Bush in his State of the Union speech on January 31, 1990; six months later, the National Education Goals Panel (NEGP) was established to monitor progress toward the goals (Vinovskis, 1999).

> The national goals, as drafted, were to "guarantee an internationally competitive standard. . . . The readiness of all children to start school. The performance of students on international achievement tests, especially in math and science. The reduction of the dropout rate and the improvement of academic performance, especially among at-risk students. The functional literacy of adult Americans. The level of training necessary to guarantee a competitive workforce. The supply of qualified teachers and up-to-date technology. The establishment of safe, disciplined and drug-free schools." The statement called for annual report cards on progress toward those objectives. (Hoffman & Broder, 1989)

The six goals of the NGA Education Summit were to

1. Ensure all children start school ready to learn
2. Achieve a high school completion rate of 90%
3. Improve achievement for all Americans in all basic subjects
4. Make American students first in the world in math and science

5. Ensure that all adults were literate and have access to lifelong learning opportunities
6. Make all schools safe, disciplined, and drug-free

The promised "restructuring" of the education system recommended by the NGA would be done entirely at the state and local level. The summit blessed several alternative and possibly conflicting approaches, to help make sure local control was a possibility. One possibility allowed parents to choose the schools their children attended, a strategy the administration planned to push at cross-country hearings.

Another approach was "school-based management," which allowed teachers and principals greater control of budgets and programs. Allowing teachers and principals more control was a favorite of education reformers. A third new approach was alternate certification of teachers, a device some states used to bring in skilled professionals who lack education degrees. Finally, the NGA proposed the introduction of incentive payments for successful schools and teachers and some unspecified form of punishment for those that fail (Hoffman & Broder, 1989).

The governors acknowledged that the process of reforming schools would take at least five years and more money. They also recognized that they would have to form partnerships with educators and other reform groups (Vinovskis, 1999). These goals were important to the course of education reform. "Why are educational goals important? Simply put, the citizens of any state are not likely to achieve more in education than they and their leaders expect and aim for. . . . Significant educational improvements do not just happen. They are planned and pursued," said Gov. Richard Riley, who coauthored the goals (Vinovskis, 1999). Cavazos first goal was to support these improvements.

Cavazos's second goal was to encourage school choice and participation for parents. On this point he agreed with both the Reagan administration and former Secretary Bennett. Cavazos intended to visit schools and talk to teachers, as Bennett had, but Cavazos was seen as less outspoken and less confrontational than his predecessor. Cavazos recognized that solving the problems of the educationally disadvantaged would take a multiyear partnership between government, educators, and the American public. "You have to involve the parents in this problem, you have to involve teachers and administrators and all the rest of it," he said, "I don't have a solution. A solution really must come from a lot of sources" (Miller, 1988; Associated Press, 2022).

This second goal for Cavazos's term as secretary of education fell under the general umbrella of increased parental choice and involvement. In line with Reagan and Bush, Cavazos supported that these changes needed to come at the state and local levels. But the government is only one small part of the equation, he emphasized, saying, "This place should not be dictating curriculum or specifics" (Miller, 1988). While Cavazos agreed with Bennett and Reagan on the need to better support teachers, improve curriculum for students from disadvantaged backgrounds, and make schools safe and drug-free, he did not agree with their approach to student loans.

Secretary Cavazos made a review of the higher-education law a priority for the department. This higher-education review was something that other secretaries had not done (DeLoughry, 1990). Cavazos's third goal was to defend the student loan programs. During his tenure Cavazos had to contend with a student federal loan problem, as loan default rates were up to 15%. Cavazos put in place new regulations for student aid eligibility and created a focus on schools who had default rates of over 60% as opposed to the 20% proposed by Bennett (DeLoughry, 1990).

In addition to supporting these three main goals, Cavazos had other efforts to pursue in his role as secretary. In 1989, Cavazos brought attention to the conditions of American Indian schools (Pitsch, 1990). In April 1989, Secretary Cavazos and Secretary of the Interior Lujan made visits to five tribal schools. While Cavazos was secretary 75% of students at tribal schools dropped out of school before graduating (Miller, 1989).

The secretary's goal was to assess the state of Indigenous education in this country. He wanted to find some things that work and move those good programs into other areas so the rest of the nation can benefit from them, Mr. Cavazos told reporters. Cavazos called for stepped-up efforts to involve parents in their children's education in the tribal schools and urged school officials to forge partnerships with local industry and higher education institutions.

While the visits garnered much public attention, some tribal members considered it a publicity stunt. Other public opinion saw it as an attempt to manage opinions about Bureau of Indian Affairs (BIA) schools. This was damage control in response to a report that had recently come out about sexual assault at BIA schools (Miller, 1989). Other than a record of a trip to five tribal schools, there are no other accounts of changes or attention toward Indigenous education.

Cavazos did a more effective job directing attention to Hispanic education. In September 1989, he called the dropout rate among Hispanic students "a national tragedy" (Pratt, 2022). "Warning that 'we can't afford to waste a whole generation' of Hispanic Americans, President Bush . . . signed an executive order that creates an advisory panel on their education and directs federal agencies to help advance their educational opportunities" (Pitsch, 1990).

Cavazos chaired the Task Force on Hispanic Education, which led to George H. W. Bush's executive order on excellence in education for Hispanic Americans (Education Week Library Staff, 2022). The advisory commission, which consisted of education, business, and civic leaders appointed by the president, advised Dr. Cavazos. "We must help education to help our Hispanic children be prepared to take their rightful place at the American table of opportunity," Cavazos said while promoting the White House Initiative on Educational Excellence for Hispanic Americans.

The Initiative on Educational Excellence for Hispanic Americans was housed in the Education Department and was to support the advisory commission. The committee worked to boost parental involvement, improve early-childhood education, and break down barriers to education and employment. In announcing his action, Mr. Bush noted that Hispanics are the nation's fastest-growing ethnic minority and said he hoped the creation of an advisory commission on Education Excellence for Hispanic Americans would ensure that their education is a national "priority" (Pitsch, 1990).

IN THE NEWS AT THIS TIME

Although Cavazos was in office for a short period, a lot happened in the States and in the world during this time. The US and Canada reached a free trade agreement. *Pan-Am 103* was blown up by terrorists and became known as the Lockerbie bombing. President Bush beat candidate Michael Dukakis for the presidency. Compact discs outsold vinyl records for the first time ever. The Ayatollah Khomeini declared author Salman Rushdie's book *The Satanic Verses* offensive and sentenced him to death. Tens of thousands of students in Beijing, China, overtook Tiananmen Square.

The Berlin Wall was opened to the West. The first world wide web server and browser was developed. Ollie North was convicted. These major changes impacted the public by creating an increased focus on individual rights and government mistrust worldwide. While the toppling of the Berlin Wall was the symbolic end of the cold war, the activities in China and the Middle East continued to impact public opinion about government overreach.

This impact on public opinion and politics created a situation for Lauro Cavazos from which he could not recover. There are questions and rumors that Cavazos was asked to resign because he was not completing his duties well (Associated Press, 2022). Others claimed he was "too low-key" (DeLoughry, 1990), especially working for a president who was promoting himself as the "education president."

Lauro Cavazos resigned his position as secretary of education in December 1990 (Education Week Library Staff, 2022). Olson and Miller (1991) said, "Unfortunately, Cavazos's inexperience in politics as well as his inability or unwillingness to be an effective educational spokesperson limited his impact and led to his eventual firing in December 1990."

Some accounts indicate that Cavazos was asked to resign during a staff meeting and other accounts suggest the resignation was his idea. Cavazos gave no reasons for his departure in his letter of resignation. Regardless, he holds a position in history, not only as a secretary of education but as the first Hispanic cabinet member (Pratt, 2022). Cavazos was widely praised for filling the top posts in the Education Department with people who were generally considered to be highly qualified (Education Week Library Staff, 2022).

Cavazos had fostered a cooperative relationship between the department and the college campuses that had not existed during the tenure of his predecessor, William J. Bennett. In addition, Cavazos highlighted issues facing students from Hispanic backgrounds; he called the dropout rate among Hispanic students "a national tragedy" in September 1989 (Associated Press, 2022). He returned to Tufts School of Medicine following his resignation. Cavazos died March 15, 2022.

Chapter 5

Lamar Alexander
1991–1993

> *If we trust parents to choose child care for their children, and we trust them to help their children choose a college to attend—and both those systems have been so successful—why do we not also trust them to choose the best elementary or high school for their children?*
>
> —Lamar Alexander

> *The chamber [of commerce] is local, and its members understand that the world is changing and that education must change as well.*
>
> —Lamar Alexander

Lamar Alexander was born on July 3, 1940, in Maryville, Tennessee. Alexander came from a family of educators. Alexander's father was an elementary school principal and later served on the local school board, while his mother ran a day care and preschool (Finn, 2022). Alexander graduated with his undergraduate degree from Vanderbilt and later went on to get his law degree from New York University Law School. Alexander was governor of Tennessee from 1979 until 1987 (Education Week Library Staff, 2017b). He was president of the University of Tennessee from 1988 to 1991, before accepting the role of secretary of education in 1991.

Lamar Alexander was sworn in as secretary of education on March 22, 1991. In his remarks from the swearing in ceremony, President Bush said of Alexander,

> Lamar Alexander understands that real reform, real restructuring of American education can only take place at the State and local level.... He knows the key to success is to make certain education reform is national, not Federal.

Nationally, we have established goals. We're setting standards, establishing priorities, and in the process, we're raising expectations. We must bring all levels of government and all Americans together—parents, teachers, students, civic and business leaders, and all interested citizens—to achieve our goals.

The announcement of Alexander as secretary of education was met with rave support from the public. "In my view, he's the first real Secretary of Education," said Denis Doyle, a senior fellow at the Hudson Institute. "Finally, we have what I would view as a genuine effort to appoint a mainstream person with superb education credentials, a genuine education agenda, and no personal ax to grind" (Miller, 1991).

Jeanne Allen, education analyst for the Heritage Foundation added: "He [Alexander] has an enormous head start, because he knows everything from the buzzwords to the players. It's also important that he is a former governor at a time when governors are playing a crucial role in education reform."

Lamar Alexander was "an education governor" (Finn, 2022). He believed that the best way to change the economic conditions in his state was to improve the education system. Alexander added to his reputation as the education governor of Tennessee when, as part of the National Governors Association, he helped reach the education guidelines that became the basis for the National Educational Goals Panel (Vinovskis, 1999).

Secretary Alexander is best known in his home state for the reform package he called the "Better Schools Program." While the program got mixed reviews, the main point of concern was a "career ladder" that allows teachers evaluated as "outstanding" to earn as much as $7,000 a year more than their peers (Miller, 1991). "Many teachers feel that what's evaluated is irrelevant to what they're doing."

"Governor Alexander has a distinguished record in education, and earned bipartisan respect for his role in stimulating education reform in the states," said Senator Edward M. Kennedy, the Massachusetts Democrat who chaired the Labor and Human Resources Committee. Alexander's support from the National Education Association was "lukewarm" as the union and he had not always agreed. Alexander's support from President Bush was warmer than lukewarm.

"Alexander enjoys the President's full support and confidence. He often confers with the President, and he is respected by his colleagues in the Cabinet" (Bell & Elmquist, 1992). Alexander supported school choice and higher educational standards. In a time of increased reporting and educational measurement, academic test scores were not promising. In 1991, the College Board reported that the average verbal score on the Scholastic Aptitude Test (SAT) hit an all-time low. The first annual "report card" on the national education goals concluded that the nation had met few of the goals.

Alexander supported the expansion of the National Assessment of Educational Progress (NAEP) to allow for academic test score comparisons at the state and local levels. He also favored school choice policies that would allow private organizations to operate public schools (Education Week Library Staff, 2017b). As a result of these measurement and testing concerns in 1991, the White House announced the launch of America 2000.

America 2000 was the result of brainstorming by Lamar Alexander, Chester E. Finn, David Kearns, Bruno V. Manno, and Scott Hamilton. A reform plan was created (Finn, 2022). President Bush and Secretary of Education Lamar Alexander unveiled this national education strategy, which included proposals for "a new generation of American schools," and a system of national tests.

In June 1991, the White House launched the New American Schools Development Corporation, a nonprofit, business-led group seeking to raise $150 million to $200 million in private money to finance research in support of President Bush's education-reform plan (U.S. Department of Education, 1991; "Remembering 1991," 1992). The funding was to support thirty government research and development teams which were to create the blueprint for the new American school (Bell & Elmquist, 1992).

AMERICA 2000

America 2000 was a long-term national strategy, not a federal program, designed to accomplish by the year 2000 the six national education goals articulated by the president and the state governors at the 1989 Education Summit in Charlottesville, Virginia (U.S. Department of Education, 1991). It contained a track for "today's students and a track for tomorrow's students" (Bell & Elmquist, 1992). The Department of Education articulated the goals of America 2000 by stating,

> By 2000, we've got to, first, ensure that every child start school ready to learn: second one, raise the high school graduation rate to 90 percent: the third one, ensure that each American student leaving the 4th, 8th and 12th grades can demonstrate competence in core subjects: four make our students first in the world in math and science achievements; fifth, ensure that every American adult is literate and has the skills necessary to compete in a global economy and exercise the rights and responsibilities of citizenship, and sixth, liberate every American school from drugs and violence so that schools encourage learning. (U.S. Department of Education, 1991)

House and Senate conferees agreed on a $31.5 billion funding bill for the Education Department for fiscal year 1992. In addition, a House committee passed legislation authorizing the development of national subject-matter standards, but not the creation of a national testing system, which provoked a presidential-veto threat from Secretary of Education Lamar Alexander ("Remembering 1992," 1993).

There was concern about the success of the program. As former Secretary Bell aptly stated, "[W]ith so many levels of government involved, the complications are enormous" (Bell & Elmquist, 1992). Bush and Alexander tried to address this issue by creating partnerships with local communities in a program that identified communities as "American 2000 Communities." America 2000 Communities agreed to adopt and support the goals of America 2000 and encouraged chambers of commerce to adopt education reform goals. This movement capitalized on Alexander's ability to create partnerships.

The criticisms of America 2000 were that, as laudable as it was, the program neglected to support and focus on the 43 million students that were in school at the time (Bell & Elmquist, 1992). It focused only on future students and partnerships and did not address the academic and social issues that were becoming more obvious. As an example, on the socioeconomic desegregation front, school officials in La Crosse, Wisconsin, proposed what was thought to be the first student-assignment plan in the nation to place students in certain schools explicitly for the sake of achieving socioeconomic balance. La Crosse officials moved students so school demographics had a balance of students from lower and higher socioeconomic groups.

In higher education, discussions about race and college admissions continued. Moving to resolve an issue raised by the Education Department's civil rights chief a year earlier, Secretary Alexander declared that most college scholarships awarded on the basis of race were illegal ("Remembering 1991," 1992). It became apparent that while test scores were a concern, people had other concerns within the schools. Alexander continued to have strong opinions. Alexander left the secretary position following Bush's loss to Bill Clinton in 1992, but his work in the political sector continued.

IN THE NEWS AT THIS TIME (1991–1993)

Congress allowed troops to use force to remove Iraqi forces from Kuwait. Operation Desert Storm began, and after many battles the Gulf War ended. Exxon agreed to pay $1 billion to clean up the oil spill of the *Exxon Valdez* in Alaska. Georgia declared independence from the Soviet Union. Queen Elizabeth II became the first British monarch to address Congress. The Warsaw Pact dissolved, and Yeltsin was elected president of the USSR.

The Crown Height riots occurred for three days in Brooklyn, New York. Estonia, Moldova, Lithuania, Tajikistan, Ukraine, and Latvia declared their independence from Russia. Russia declared independence from the Soviets and the USSR dissolved. There were fires in California. Magic Johnson announced he had HIV and retired from basketball. Armenian citizens were massacred by their armed forces, and South Africa voted to end apartheid.

The Great Chicago Flood devastated Chicago. Riots in Los Angeles, California, lasted 53 days following the acquittal of police officers charged with excessive force in the beating of Rodney King. An arms reduction act was signed by Bush and Yeltsin. The year 1992 saw Hurricane Andrew and the advent of *Mario Kart*. Manuel Noriega was sentenced in the US for drug trafficking and money laundering. The first smartphone was introduced by IBM. This time period contained the seeds of things that continue—racial tensions and riots, Russian state politics, and standards-based education reform promoted by President Bush.

Chapter 6

Richard Riley
1993–2001

We must look at the stark reality that there is a continuing achievement gap between the rich and the poor, and between whites and minority students. . . . This gap is a gaping hole in our commitment to fulfilling the American promise, and it will only get bigger if we do not close the digital divide as well.

—Richard Riley

[O]nly half of all parents are reading to their children every day. My message to parents is to read, read, read. It makes a powerful difference.

—Richard Riley

If there's something you believe in, you never lose. . . . You might be delayed, but you never lose.

—Richard Riley

President Clinton chose Richard Wilson Riley to be secretary of education in December 1992 (U.S. Department of Education, "Richard W. Riley"). Richard "Dick" Riley was the sixth secretary of education. He held the position of department secretary from 1993 until 2001, tying with Arne Duncan as having the longest tenure of any secretary of education (Dodge, 2002). Clinton knew Riley because of the work they did together as governors, specifically the work of the National Governors Association that became America 2000.

According to the *Christian Science Monitor*, many Americans regard Dick Riley as "one of the great statesmen of education in this century." David Broder, columnist for the *Washington Post*, has called him one of the "most decent and honorable people in public life." It has also been observed that Riley had a knack for being chosen for things (Chebatoris, 2012).

Richard Wilson Riley was born in Greenville County, South Carolina, on January 2, 1933. He graduated cum laude from Furman University in 1954 and served as an officer in the U.S. Navy. In 1959, Riley received a law degree from the University of South Carolina. (Ed Week Library Staff, 2017c). Riley married Ann Osteen Yarborough and they have four children and fourteen grandchildren. Richard Riley was a state representative and state senator from 1963 until 1977, was elected governor in 1978, and then reelected in 1982.

Riley was governor of South Carolina for two terms prior to joining the Clinton administration as secretary of education. As governor, Riley focused heavily on education and passed the Education Improvement Act (1984), which overhauled the public school system in the state. On being governor, Riley observed that "my most successful thing was getting elected." An astute observation, indeed, by the man for whom the state's Constitution was changed so that he could serve a second term as governor (Chebatoris, 2012).

Riley's goals as secretary included:

- Help all children to master the basics of reading and math
- Make schools safer
- Reduce class sizes in grades 1–3
- Help states and schools to hire 100,000 more good teachers
- Modernize and build new schools to meet record-breaking student enrollments
- Help students learn to use computers
- Expand after-school programs (U.S. Dept of Ed, Riley)

Riley supported standards. Since the mid-1980s he had supported the movement to identify what a child should know at various grades and in various subjects. During Clinton's first term, Riley helped launch historic initiatives to raise academic standards and to improve instruction for the poor and disadvantaged.

Secretary Riley moved to expand grant and loan programs, which he believed would help more Americans go to college. Riley wanted to prepare young people for the world of work and to improve teaching (U.S. Dept of Ed, Riley). He also believed that the Department of Education should have a leading role in technology. The Goals 2000: Educate America Act was signed by President Clinton and authorized $5 million to create a technology office within the department and underwrite state planning grants to promote the use of technology in reform (West, 1994).

Riley said that "cooperative efforts between the public and private sectors would be vital to achieving the vision of access to telecommunications for all" (West, 1994). Educational access to the internet and other electronic networks was a central goal of the administration's National Information Infrastructure Initiative, which had been championed by Vice President Gore. The year 1994 saw the opening of the first synchronous online high school (Thompson, 2021).

Riley operated well in Washington. He was a soft-spoken man, but he got things done. Riley believed "partnership works better than partisanship and really coming together in kind of a consensus of what works best." He believed that both sides could work together, even if one had tried to abolish the other. "I always prided myself on bringing in top people and making sure I had a diverse group" (Fox, 2011).

There were some bumps in the road to partnership. During Riley's term, Newt Gingrich proposed the "Contract with America," which resurrected the idea of abolishing the department (Dodge, 2002). "[W]e had a rough period during '95 and '96 [with] the effort to do away with the Department—but coming out of that we have had tremendous support," said Riley. He was proud of the efforts he and the president made and at the time declared, "[T]his last budget is the best budget education has ever had in the history of the country, and it's been bipartisan" (Ed Week Library Staff, 2017c).

Highlights of Riley's tenure:

- Created the Federal Communications Commission's E-rate program, which allowed schools and libraries to receive discounted internet and telephone rates.
- Advocated for technology in the classroom.
- Convened the first Secretary's Conference on Educational Technology.
- Issued the first federal grants to charter schools. (Pitsch, 1995)

Goals 2000, also known as the Educate America Act, was focused on standards. It was a movement toward uniform academic standards from state to state, with state control; federal dollars would go to the states to assist in getting their standards movement in place. All 50 states, in one way or another, were involved in standards (Suarez, 2001).

There was, as in previous decades, concern about government overreach associated with federal funding of state initiatives. Senate hearings initially indicated that rather than start a new program, the government should divert funding to the IDEA, which had never been federally funded to the level that was promised (Congress of the U.S., 1995).

> Goals 2000 provides support to States, local communities and schools to help design and implement the school improvements most needed in that particular State or community it is grassroots, bottom-up reform. Goals 2000 creates a partnership between the Federal Government and States and communities working to improve their schools. Goals2000 asks States to (1) set challenging academic standards; (2) develop their own comprehensive education reforms; and (3) do this with broad-based grassroots parental involvement. In return, the Federal Government provides funds and flexibility. Ninety percent of the dollars that this Subcommittee appropriates for Goals2000 flows to local school districts and schools. (Congress of the U.S., 1995)

Goals 2000 was signed into law in March of 1994.

The time Riley dedicated to education was successful. Based on his goals, Riley did well by the students in South Carolina and across the nation.

> "Dick Riley's commitment to South Carolina's children, and to our nation's children," says Joe Waters, associate director at the Institute for Child Success, an education advocacy organization in Greenville, "is incredible not only for its depth, but for its longevity. For the better part of the last half-century, Secretary Riley has been a committed public servant and advocate working to ensure that every child born in South Carolina and across this country has a fair opportunity to succeed in school, in the workforce, and to contribute to a prosperous society. He is an inspiration to all of us who strive to make our own contributions to a brighter South Carolina because he has shown us that we must remain committed to this cause over the course of a whole career, not just for a season of life." (Chebatoris, 2012)

With the change in presidency, Riley stepped down. He believed he handed the department in good condition to Rod Paige and that Paige would be a good secretary of education. Riley and Paige were friends. They worked together on many educational issues (Suarez, 2001). Riley was happy to have been secretary and he loved all of it, almost. He was not a fan of the politics. When he left, his work in education continued.

In recognition of his lifelong dedication to education, there are three educational institutions named in Riley's honor: the Richard W. Riley Institute of Government, Politics and Public Leadership at his alma mater, Furman University; the Richard W. Riley College of Education at Winthrop University; and the Richard W. Riley College of Education and Leadership at Walden University in Naples, Florida (Chebatoris, 2012).

IN THE NEWS

During the time Riley was in office, 1993–2001, there were great changes in technology and the international/national climate. It is a challenge to concisely list the events of eight years. Internationally, it was a time of reorganizing—from Ireland to the Middle East and the Eastern Block to the Philippines, boundaries and regimes were being challenged and redrawn. There were plane crashes and hijackings. In the US, legislation had the headlines, along with world wide web firsts and standoffs between militant factions and government officials.

Technology was just hitting the national scene, as noted by Riley's education goals. The country knew that technology was the future but in the year 2000, just less than half the homes in the country had internet and the internet was not mobile, it was hardwired into computers at a desk. Flip phones were all the rage and texting happened a few letters at a time. Dolly the sheep was the first mammal cloned from a cell. Cyber hacking began with the first public incident being the "Melissa worm" in 1999. Microsoft was found to have violated antitrust laws.

Nationally, Janet Reno was sworn in as the first female attorney general. There was a standoff at Waco, Texas, and a landmark prison riot in Ohio. The North American Free Trade Agreement passed. The Brady Bill was signed into law. North Korea and the United States signed an agreement that required North Korea to stop its nuclear weapons program and agree to inspections.

Mississippi finally abolished slavery and ratified the thirteenth amendment (1995). The Oklahoma City bombing killed 168 people. The Gulf War ended with Operation Desert Storm. The Communications Decency Act was passed by Congress. Montana Freemen had an 81-one day standoff against the FBI. The Centennial Park bombing occurred in Atlanta. The House of Representatives voted to reprimand Speaker of the House Newt Gingrich.

Tiger Woods was the youngest player to ever win the Masters golf tournament. The US established sanctions against Sudan for human rights violations. The Clinton-Lewinsky sex scandal took to the news. The U.S. auto workers strikes occurred. There was another shooting in the Capitol. Google was founded in 1998. LGBT rights took the headlines. Bill Clinton was the second president in history to be impeached; he was subsequently acquitted.

Internationally, Czechoslovakia dissolved. The Bosnian war began, and the World Trade Center in New York City was bombed. There were many bombings by the Irish Republican Army (IRA) in Ireland and London, but the IRA eventually called a ceasefire and signed a peace treaty. Israeli prime minister Yitzhak Rabin shook hands with Palestine Liberation Organization chairman

Yasser Arafat at the White House after signing the Oslo Accords and thus began a series of PLO/Israeli discussions.

Mongolia held its first elections. The European Union was formed. Israel and Vatican City established diplomatic relations. The Rwandan genocide occurred. The Channel Tunnel, aka the Chunnel, opened between France and the United Kingdom. The First, and then Second, Chechen war began. The Croatian war began. The Bosnian war ended. The city of Bethlehem moved from Israeli to Palestinian control. The Lebanon war ended.

The Taliban captured Kabul, Afghanistan. Football (soccer) fans went crazy and games became dangerous, as fights and stampedes injured stadium goers. A 36-year Guatemalan civil war ended, but massacres began in Algeria. China took control of Hong Kong. Princess Diana was killed in a car accident. A war started and ended in the Congo. All handguns were banned in Great Britain.

The Olympics happened—all of the times they are supposed to and an American was the youngest female to ever win a figure skating gold medal. Clinton imposed trade and economic sanctions against the Taliban, specifically the Taliban in Afghanistan. Overall, online and in the world, boundaries are being explored, individuals are demanding their rights, and the education climate begins to reflect these changes.

Chapter 7

Rod Paige
2001–2005

Education is the only business still debating the usefulness of technology.

—Rod Paige

The NEA is a terrorist organization.

—Rod Paige

To put it simply, we need to keep the arts in education because they instill in students the habits of mind that last a lifetime: critical analysis skills, the ability to deal with ambiguity and to solve problems, perseverance and a drive for excellence. Moreover, the creative skills children develop through the arts carry them toward new ideas, new experiences, and new challenges, not to mention personal satisfaction. This is the intrinsic value of the arts, and it cannot be overestimated.

—Rod Paige

On January 21, 2001, the U.S. Senate confirmed Dr. Rod Paige as the seventh U.S. secretary of education (U.S. Department of Education, "Rod Paige"). Paige served as secretary of education under President George W. Bush from 2001 until 2005. Bush selected Paige for the good work he did in the Houston Public Schools.

Roderick "Rod" Raynor Paige was born June 17, 1933, in Monticello, Mississippi. Growing up, Paige persevered through a still segregated school system. He was the oldest of five children. His father, Raynor Paige, was a public school principal, and his mother, Sophie Paige, was a public school librarian (Marzell, 2018). Paige earned a bachelor's degree from Jackson State University in his home state. He then earned both a master's and a doctoral degree from Indiana University. He is a veteran and served as a medical corpsman in the U.S. Navy from 1955 until 1957.

Paige began working with students early in his career as a teacher and a coach. He then served for a decade as dean of the College of Education at Texas Southern University (TSU). As dean, Paige worked to ensure that future educators would receive the training and expertise necessary to succeed in the classroom. He also established the university's Center for Excellence in Urban Education, a research facility that concentrates on issues related to instruction and management in urban school systems (U.S. Department of Education, "Rod Paige").

In 1994, Paige became superintendent of Houston Independent School District (HISD), the nation's seventh largest school district. Paige was named one of "Houston's 25 most powerful people" in guiding the city's growth and prosperity. In 2001, he was named National Superintendent of the Year by the American Association of School Administrators. Paige was the first secretary of education to have been a superintendent. He was the first African American to serve as the secretary of education (Marzell, 2018).

The results that Paige saw were touted as the "Texas Miracle" (Leung, 2004). As superintendent, Paige created the Peer Examination, Evaluation, and Redesign (PEER) program, which solicited recommendations from business and community professionals for strengthening school support services and programs.

Paige started a system of charter schools that have broad authority in decisions regarding staffing, textbooks, and materials. He saw to it that HISD paid teachers salaries that were competitive with those offered by other large Texas school districts. Paige made HISD the first school district in the state to institute performance contracts modeled on those in the private sector, whereby senior staff members' continued employment with HISD is based on their performance.

Rod Paige was given credit for the schools' success by making principals and administrators accountable for how well their students did (Leung, 2004). He also introduced teacher incentive pay, which rewards teachers for raising test scores. While controversy arose about possible reporting discrepancies that may have made Paige look more miraculous, the work that he did in Texas drew great national attention (Leung, 2004).

Upon taking office, Paige learned of wide-scale criminal fraud, waste, and abuse within the department that was featured on national network news. In response to this abuse, Paige made improving management one of his priorities. Paige rallied the department to create the Blueprint for Management Excellence in order to build an organization worthy of the taxpayers' trust and the president's vision (U.S. Department of Education, "Rod Paige"). This sense of accountability and stewardship was the way he approached education in the Houston schools and the way he approached it in his federal role.

The driving force behind Paige's work as secretary was his shared belief with President Bush that education is a civil right, just like the right to vote or to be treated equally. Paige also believed it was wrong to fight discrimination with discrimination. For that reason, he strongly supported the president's vision of affirmative access that promoted diversity in our nation's colleges and universities through race-neutral alternatives (U.S. Department of Education, "Rod Paige").

This commitment made Paige a strong ally in the work that he and the president would do together in forwarding the accountability of the department. This accountability applied to the support of school vouchers, which had been a point of discussion for many years in the department. "Paige said private-school vouchers in the District of Columbia amount to nothing short of 'emancipation' for hundreds of poor and minority students, allowing them to 'throw off the chains of a school system that has not served them well'" (Associated Press, 2004).

This support of vouchers put Paige at odds with unions and interest groups, but it would not be the hallmark of his time at the department. Paige presided over the biggest federal shakeup to education in a generation, a law demanding that schools show improvement among all students, regardless of race or wealth (U.S. Department of Education, "Rod Paige").

Each of the seven secretaries of education prior to Paige contributed to the department's current stature and influence in policy making (Stallings, 2002). Former secretaries such as Cavazos began to move in this direction with his emphasis on accountability, but when asked, Cavazos and Hufstedler, although concerned with standards, were worried about the high stakes attached to testing (Dodge, 2002) and the lack of emphasis on character development.

The No Child Left Behind Act (NCLB) of 2001 was a U.S. federal law aimed at improving public primary and secondary schools, and thus student performance via increased accountability for schools, school districts, and states (Nolen & Duignan, 2021). The law passed with bipartisan support in December of 2001 and was signed into law in January 2002. Law passage relied heavily on bipartisan support between Sec. Rod Paige and Sen. Edward Kennedy of Massachusetts.

One of the key factors in the passage of NCLB was Paige's ability to sway senators from the opposing party (Dodge, 2002). Sandy Kress, a former senior education adviser to Bush said that Paige had "spoken with great moral authority about the goals of No Child Left Behind. He feels it personally. He brought a history, he brought experience, and I think he brought a great commitment to the cause" (Associated Press, 2004).

The signing of the No Child Left Behind Act of 2001 signified a clear shift from the department's early role as data keeper and dispenser of student aid funds to its emergent role as an education policymaker and reformer (Dodge, 2002). Under the law, states were required to administer yearly tests of the reading and mathematics skills of public school students and to demonstrate adequate progress toward raising the scores of all students to a level defined as "proficient" or higher by 2014 (Nolen & Duignan, 2021).

The No Child Left Behind Act reauthorized the Elementary and Secondary Education Act (ESEA) of 1965. This reauthorization was called "the most far-reaching reform of the nation's public education system since the creation of the department (Dodge, 2002). The goals of NCLB were closing the achievement gap for disadvantaged students, improving teacher preparation and rewards, and instituting closely monitored accountability systems for all (Dodge, 2002).

Paige, who grew up in segregated Mississippi, put No Child Left Behind in the category of *Brown v. Board of Education*, the landmark case that ended the practice of separating schools by race (Associated Press, 2004). He compared critics of the administration's education overhaul to those who opposed school desegregation 50 years ago, saying both will fall on the wrong side of history. As part of the authorization of this law, there was an over 20% increase in the education budget over the previous year.

Paige resigned from his position of secretary of education on November 15, 2004. The legacy of NCLB is still felt in education today. Based on interviews and reports, Paige supported the legislation because he believed it was the way to help all students succeed. Former Secretary of Education Bennett called Paige an "in-the-trenches reformer" (Associated Press, 2004).

IN THE NEWS 2001–2005

The first thing that comes to mind when reviewing the events from 2001 to 2005 is the destruction of the twin towers of the World Trade Center in New York City by two hijacked planes, while a third smashed into the Pentagon in Arlington County, Virginia, and a fourth crashed into a field near Shanksville, Pennsylvania. Paige was sitting with George W. Bush at the Emma E. Booker Elementary School in Sarasota, Florida, when Bush received the news that a second plane had hit the World Trade Center on September 11, 2001. Following an emergency press conference called by the president, Paige and the lieutenant governor of Florida proceeded with their discussion of education (Bush, 2001).

The Mars Odyssey was launched, the United States lost its seat on the United Nation Human Rights Commission, NATO sent a peacekeeping force into Yugoslavia, and Tropical Storm Allison became the costliest storm in U.S. history (Events History, 2014).

In November 2001, the "War on Terrorism" officially began. Taiwan became Taipei, China. Bush called Iraq, Iran, and North Korea the "Axis of Evil." In March 2002, the US invaded Afghanistan and troops would remain there until removed in 2021. The Moscow Treaty was signed, and Switzerland joined the United Nations. The first version of Mozilla Firefox was launched. Enron chief Andrew Fastow was indicted.

A blackout hit Canada and northeastern United States. The foreign minister of Sweden was stabbed and died. Former president of Iraq Saddam Hussein was captured. There was a coup in Haiti. Ireland became the first country to ban smoking. Google announced Gmail. The last episode of *Friends* aired. The first same-sex marriages were performed.

Chapter 8

Margaret Spellings
2005–2009

We cannot prepare students for the global economy if we don't get them to grade level first.

—Margaret Spellings

I mean, one thing I know about change is we are not going to close the achievement gap without educators.

—Margaret Spellings

Higher education is confronting challenges, like the economy is, about the need for a higher number of more adequately trained, more highly educated citizenry.

—Margaret Spellings

We want to obviously foster a relationship that we're a partner with states; that we all share the same goals of closing the achievement gap, just as the Congress does; and that we're practical and sophisticated enough to understand what they're talking about.

—Margaret Spellings

Margaret Spellings was U.S. secretary of education from 2005 to 2009. In that role, she oversaw an agency with a nearly $70 billion budget and more than 10,000 employees and contractors. As a member of the president's cabinet, she led the implementation of the No Child Left Behind Act

(NCLB), a historic national initiative to provide enhanced accountability for the education of 50 million U.S. public school students. As the first mother of school-aged children to serve as education secretary, Spellings had a special appreciation for the hopes and concerns of American families (U.S. Department of Education, "Margaret Spellings").

Margaret Spellings was born Margaret M. Dudar on November 30, 1957, in Ann Arbor, Michigan. Dudar moved with her family from Michigan to Texas where she finished her K–12 education and graduated from high school. She graduated from the University of Houston with a bachelor's degree in political science. Spellings has been married twice and has two daughters.

> Spellings worked as an aide in the legislature and was a lobbyist for the Texas school boards association. Karl Rove, a political adviser to George W. Bush, introduced Bush to Spellings, needed advice on education issues. Bush was impressed with Spellings and made her political director of his 1994 campaign for governor. Spellings worked as Governor Bush's chief education advisor until he became president in 2001. (Encyclopedia.com, 2018a)

Spellings was senior adviser to then-governor George W. Bush of Texas, led governmental and external relations for the Texas Association of School Boards, and has served in key positions at Austin Community College and with the Texas legislature.

When Bush became president in 2001, he brought Spellings to Washington with him. Spellings served as assistant to the president for domestic policy, where she helped create the No Child Left Behind Act and crafted policies on education, immigration, health care, labor, transportation, justice, housing, and other elements of the president's domestic agenda (U.S. Department of Education, "Margaret Spellings").

Spellings was appointed secretary of education following the resignation of Secretary Rod Paige. Her biggest accomplishment was helping to pass the No Child Left Behind Act in January of 2002 (Encyclopedia.com, 2018a). Paige, Bush, and Spellings worked to get the controversial act passed. Spellings's main goal as secretary was to fully implement the controversial standards of Bush's signature education reform. Once implemented, Spellings was intent to allow for more flexibility in how the act is enforced at the local level without bargaining away its essential parts (Encyclopedia.com, 2018a).

Spellings had support from the president to see what was and was not working in NCLB and make changes where necessary. "In January, I indicated that the secretary should move forward on reforms she can undertake administratively if Congress fails to act," President Bush said in a statement released by the White House (DuBose, 2008). One of the big problems on the road to accountability was that while the initial draft left great flexibility to the states, it neglected to take into consideration the need to be able to compare uniform data.

"Secretary Spellings announced a package of regulations and pilot programs that were to address the dropout crisis in America, strengthen accountability, improve the lowest-performing schools and ensure that more students get access to high-quality tutoring" (DuBose, 2008). "States were to be required to use a uniform method of calculating graduation rates by the 2012–13 school year," Education Secretary Margaret Spellings said in announcing proposed revisions to federal education regulations (DuBose, 2008). Under the proposed plan, only students who completed school on time with a regular degree will be counted as graduates, which would eliminate students who take additional time or who acquire an alternative to a diploma, such as a GED certificate.

Sen. Edward M. Kennedy (D-Mass.), who cosponsored the No Child Left Behind Act in 2001, urged Bush "to reverse course in his tin-cup education budget and finally invest in the education of our children." In a statement released by Kennedy's office, he praised some of Spellings's proposals as "important improvements for implementing No Child Left Behind. . . . No Child Left Behind is here to stay, but states and local districts that show measurable student achievement were to have more flexibility in how the law is implemented" (Norris, 2005).

Instead of creating a national requirement for improvement based on the rates compiled through the new method, Spellings's proposals allowed states to set their own improvement goals. The proposed changes also called for schools to take greater initiative in informing parents of free tutoring programs available for low-income students in underperforming schools.

Secretary Spellings believed we must not retreat from the world in the face of increased competition. She began during her time in the Governor's office with her efforts to end the practice of automatically passing students to the next grade to keep them in class with students of the same age, known as "social promotion." This resolve to make sure students know course material continued as a theme in Spellings's time as secretary. She led the effort to pass President Bush's American Competitiveness Initiative to strengthen math and science instruction and encouraged high schools to offer more rigorous and advanced coursework. Spellings worked to implement Academic Competitiveness and National SMART grants, which provided millions of dollars to low-income students who majored in math, science, or critical foreign languages (U.S. Department of Education, "Margaret Spellings"). As secretary, Spellings also convened the Commission on the Future of Higher Education to recommend reform at the postsecondary level.

IN THE NEWS 2005–2009

YouTube was launched. The Kyoto protocol was adopted. There was a lockout of the National Hockey League (NHL). The Supreme Court ruled that it was unconstitutional to execute juveniles who are found guilty of murder. Pope John Paul II died. The Syrian occupation of Lebanon ended, Hurricane Dennis hit Florida, and over 500 bombs were set off in Bangladesh by terrorists.

Hurricane Katrina wiped out parts of New Orleans. Soon after, Hurricane Rita hit, and Hurricane Wilma followed several months later. There were riots in Toledo, Ohio. Twitter launched. Serbia declared independence. Fidel Castro transferred power to his brother Raul and later retired. The National Museum of the Marine Corp was opened in Quantico, Virginia. There was a gas pipeline explosion in Nigeria. Nancy Pelosi was named the first female Speaker of the House.

The first iPhone was revealed. There was flooding in Jakarta. Israeli archaeologists discovered the tomb of Herod the Great south of Jerusalem. Russia tested the largest of all conventional weapons. There was a massacre in Omaha, Nebraska, when a gunman opened fire. There was a Super Tuesday tornado outbreak in 2008. U.S. Immigration and Customs Enforcement conducted the Postville Raid, the largest-ever raid of a workplace in Postville, Iowa, where they arrested nearly 400 immigrants for identity theft and document fraud.

There were floods in South China. The 2008 Olympics took place in Beijing, China. The U.S. government took control of the two largest mortgage companies. There were more bombings in India. The Emergency Economic Stabilization Act of 2008 for the U.S. financial system was signed by President George W. Bush. Bernie Madoff was arrested for securities fraud. This was a time of financial instability as the mortgage crisis was realized. International tensions throughout India, Russia, and in the Middle East continued.

Chapter 9

Arne Duncan
2009–2016

Education is the ultimate bipartisan, nonpartisan issue. There's nothing Republican or Democrat about more kids having access to pre-K. There's nothing Republican or Democrat about raising high school graduation rates. There's nothing liberal or conservative about having more young people prepared to go to college and being able to afford it.

—Arne Duncan

Education runs on lies.

—Arne Duncan

Secretary Arne Duncan was confirmed by the Senate on January 20, 2009. Duncan was the eleventh secretary of education and was selected by President Barack Obama (U.S. Department of Education, "Arne Duncan"). Secretary Duncan was an unwavering advocate for low-income and minority students and a longtime basketball buddy to President Barack Obama. Duncan moved aggressively to raise the academic bar in U.S. schools (Emma et al., 2015).

Arne Starkey Duncan was born November 6, 1964, in Chicago, Illinois. He was raised in Hyde Park, Chicago, which is the neighborhood near the University of Chicago. Both of Duncan's parents were educators. Duncan's mother ran an after-school program primarily serving African American youth in the nearby Kenwood neighborhood. Duncan's father was a psychology professor at the University of Chicago. As a child he attended the University of Chicago Laboratory Schools (U.S. Department of Education, "Arne Duncan").

After high school, Duncan attended Harvard University and graduated magna cum laude. From 1987 to 1991, Duncan played professional basketball in Australia, where he also worked with children who were wards of the state. Duncan is married to Karen Duncan, and they have two children (U.S. Department of Education, "Arne Duncan"). His term will be remembered for his embrace of stimulus-fueled Race to the Top grants that helped propel many of the controversial ideas he long embraced (Emma et al., 2015). Duncan was secretary of education from 2009 to 2016.

Duncan was tapped by Chicago mayor Richard Daley to run the city's schools in 2001 (Kingsbury, 2008). Duncan is credited with significantly raising student performance on national and state tests, increasing graduation rates and the numbers of students taking Advanced Placement courses, and boosting the total number of scholarships secured by CPS students to more than $150 million (U.S. Department of Education, "Arne Duncan").

Prior to joining the Chicago Public Schools, from 1992 to 1998 Duncan ran the nonprofit education foundation Ariel Education Initiative, which helped fund a college education for inner-city children under the I Have a Dream program. He served as the chief executive officer of the Chicago Public Schools (CPS) before becoming secretary of education (U.S. Department of Education, "Arne Duncan").

Duncan was particularly attuned to the achievement gap between high- and low-income students and hinted that he did not approve of the way Illinois schools received the bulk of their funding from local tax revenue. "It's morally inexcusable that children who happen to be born in wealthier communities, white ones, get a better education than those who live in poor communities. . . . Clearly, as a state, we've lacked the political courage to fundamentally challenge the status quo, not just tweak it at its edges." He added, "It doesn't need a tweak. It needs a fundamental change" (Kingsbury, 2008).

Duncan helped to secure congressional support for President Obama's investments in education, including the American Recovery and Reinvestment Act's $100 billion to fund 325,000 teaching jobs, increases in Pell grants, reform efforts such as Race to the Top and Investing in Innovation, and interventions in low-performing schools (U.S. Department of Education, "Arne Duncan"). Duncan had the president's ear; they are personal friends and often played basketball together, even on Election Day. Obama and Duncan have a lot in common. Both men were educated at Harvard and have deep Chicago roots (Kingsbury, 2008).

According to Kingsbury,

> Duncan was considered by most [in Congress] to be a quiet consensus builder. In Chicago, his knack for forging alliances could be seen in his strong relationships with the local teachers' unions despite his embrace of reforms the union

was leery of, including school choice, pay for performance and a willingness to close down failing schools. (2008)

Duncan won praise for uniting education reformers, teachers, principals, and business stakeholders behind an aggressive education reform agenda. This agenda included:

- Opening more than 100 new schools
- Expanding after school and summer learning programs
- Closing underperforming schools
- Increasing early childhood and college access
- Dramatically boosting the caliber of teachers
- Building public-private partnerships around a variety of education initiatives (U.S. Department of Education, "Arne Duncan")

Duncan clashed with many camps in the education community since taking the post of secretary of education, and he echoed Obama's frustration with what the president called "tired educational debates" (Kingsbury, 2008). "It's been Democrat vs. Republican, vouchers vs. the status quo, more money vs. more reform," Obama said. "There's partisanship and there's bickering, but no understanding that both sides have good ideas and good intentions" (Kingsbury, 2008).

During Duncan's tenure, the department launched a comprehensive effort to transform the teaching profession (U.S. Department of Education, "Arne Duncan"). Duncan supported charter schools, encouraged using testing for measuring teachers and schools, and championed the divisive Common Core standards. He took on the higher education establishment by pushing policies to regulate for-profit colleges and made colleges and universities more transparent (Emma et al., 2015).

Duncan spearheaded merit-pay incentives for both teachers and students and suggested opening the country's first gay-friendly high school (Kingsbury, 2008). Duncan secured an additional $10 billion to avoid teacher layoffs (U.S. Department of Education, "Arne Duncan"). The department focused billions of dollars to transform struggling schools, prompting nearly 1,000 low-performing schools nationwide to recruit new staff, adopt new teaching methods, and add learning time. The Race to the Top program had the incentives, guidance, and flexibility it needed to support reforms in states (U.S. Department of Education, "Arne Duncan").

Duncan's strong stances prompted delegates to the 2014 National Education Association's annual convention to pass a new business item on July 4 that called for him to resign (Loewus & Sawchuk, 2014). The surprising move came on the heels of union anger over moves across the United States to revise due-process protections, tenure, and seniority—some of which were supported by Democrats, including the Obama administration (Loewus & Sawchuk, 2014).

The California Teachers Association was frustrated with the secretary after his comments on the *Vergara v. California* ruling, which found that the state's tenure law violated student rights (Loewus & Sawchuk, 2014). In higher education, Duncan introduced the income-based repayment program, where student loan payments were reduced for college graduates in low-paying jobs and loans would be forgiven after 10 years for workers in certain public service occupations, such as teachers, police officers, and firefighters (U.S. Department of Education, "Arne Duncan").

"Education runs on lies" is the first sentence of Arne Duncan's book about how schools work. While he achieved many things in education, that sentence and his brutally honest account of education may be what he is remembered for most. Duncan's tenure as secretary was marked by a number of significant accomplishments on behalf of American students and teachers (U.S. Department of Education, "Arne Duncan").

IN THE NEWS 2009–2016

The seven years of Arne Duncan's tenure were marked by technology advances, social change, shootings, bombings, crashes, and movement from one geographic area to another. The first block of blockchain Bitcoin was established in 2009. Chrysler filed for Chapter 11. Same-sex marriage was legalized in Sweden. There were more bombings in Baghdad. Bernie Madoff pled guilty. Coal miners were killed in an explosion in West Virginia. Arab Spring and Algerian protests began.

Barack Obama announced that Osama bin Laden was killed by U.S. Navy SEALs special forces in Abbottabad, Pakistan. Oprah Winfrey aired her last show. Michael Phelps broke the record set in 1964 by Larisa Latynina for the most medals won at the Olympics. The Middle East and Gaza strip continued to be plagued with accidents and bombings. Pakistani Taliban made a failed attempt to assassinate Malala Yousafzai.

There was a shooting at Sandy Hook Elementary School in Connecticut. Disney acquired Lucas Films and the Star Wars franchise. There was a prison riot in Venezuela and a night club fire in Brazil. Pope Benedict XVI announced his resignation from the papacy and Pope Francis was elected. The Boston Marathon was bombed. Iraqi attacks increased in May 2013. The government of Detroit, Michigan, filed for bankruptcy.

Twelve people were killed in the Washington Navy Yard. In 2013, the U.S. federal government shut down nonessential services after it was unable to pass a budget measure. There were too many deaths at the hands of police officers and the Black Lives Matters movement began. There were too many earthquakes and bombings and train crashes to name. Forty-three people were killed in a mudslide in Oso, Washington. Two hundred female students went missing after a mass kidnapping in Nigeria.

The 2014 Olympics, Paralympics, and Junior Olympics took place. The office of a French satirical newspaper was attacked, prompting the world to share #JeSuisCharlie? And "I am not Charlie Hebdo." There was a shooting at a church in Charleston, and one at television news anchors in Virginia; 2015 saw at least 57 mass shootings in the United States. The European refugee crisis began as many began fleeing Syria and other areas in the Middle East and Africa. In the US, same-sex marriage was legalized nationwide.

Chapter 10

John King, Jr.
2016–2017

In a nation where there is a 30–40 point achievement gap between low-income students of color and their more affluent peers, in a nation where students with the most income are seven times more likely to go to college than students with the least, in a nation where our urban school systems have high school graduation rates around 50%, and in a nation where one in four African-American men between 19 and 29 is either in prison, on probation, or on parole, we need to bring to the work of closing the achievement gap.

—John King, Jr.

I'm the first U.S. Secretary of Education to get kicked out of high school. . . . But I hope I'm not the last, because part of why I'm standing here is because people were willing to give me a second chance. People were willing to see me as more than the sum of my mistakes. They were willing to see potential and possibility.

—John King, Jr.

Dr. John B. King Jr. was sworn in March 14, 1996, as the tenth secretary of education. President Obama called Dr. King "an exceptionally talented educator," citing his commitment to "preparing every child for success" and his lifelong dedication to education as a teacher, principal, and leader of schools and school systems (U.S. Department of Education, "John B. King, Jr."). King worked as a principal adviser to President Obama before becoming secretary.

King began his advisory work for Obama in 2015. As principal adviser, he carried out the duties of the deputy secretary, overseeing all preschool through 12th-grade education policies, programs, and strategic initiatives, as well as the operations of the department. King was asked to step up to the secretary position by President Obama after the announcement of the retirement of his predecessor, Secretary Arne Duncan (Atkinson, 2015).

John B. King, Jr., was born January 5, 1975, in New York, where he grew up in East Flatbush, Brooklyn. His parents, two New York City public school educators, believed "that school is at the heart of our promise of equality of opportunity for all Americans" (Atkinson, 2015). King's father was Brooklyn's first African American school principal, and his Puerto Rican mother was the first in her family to graduate from college (Atkinson, 2015).

Sadly, both of King's parents had died by the time he was 12. King credited his teachers for his success. King moved around a lot, living with family and friends. He eventually went to live with his father's brother, Uncle Hal, who was a career air force officer and had been a Tuskegee airman. Living with Uncle Hal and his wife, Aunt Jean, provided a sense of normalcy for King; there was dinner every night at the same time, strict rules, and high expectations. As King said, "I was back on track" (King, 2009).

King holds a bachelor of arts in government from Harvard University. He earned a JD from Yale Law School, as well as a master's in the teaching of social studies and a doctorate in education from Teachers College at Columbia University. King lives in Silver Spring, Maryland, with his wife (a former kindergarten and first grade teacher) and their two daughters (Education Trust, 2022).

Dr. King began his career in education teaching high school social studies in San Juan, Puerto Rico, and then Boston, Massachusetts. King went on to be an administrator. At 24, he cofounded Uncommon Schools, a nonprofit charter management organization that operated some of the highest-performing urban public schools in New York, New Jersey, and Massachusetts, and now has 44 institutions (Atkinson, 2015). King served as managing director with Uncommon Schools until his appointment as senior deputy commissioner at the New York State Education Department in 2009.

King was a cofounder and codirector for curriculum and instruction at Roxbury (Massachusetts) Preparatory Charter School. In 2011, Dr. King became commissioner of education for the state of New York. As commissioner, King served as chief executive officer of the state Education Department and as president of the University of the State of New York. He oversaw the state's elementary and secondary schools (serving 3.1 million students), public, independent, and proprietary colleges and universities, libraries, museums, and numerous other educational institutions.

King was one of the nation's youngest state education leaders at the time of his appointment as secretary of education and the first African American and Puerto Rican to serve. Dr. King oversaw the department's work leading cross-agency collaboration for President Obama's My Brother's Keeper task force.

My Brother's Keeper sought to address persistent opportunity gaps faced by boys and young men of color and to ensure that all young people are able to reach their full potential. Arne Duncan has said that King was more similar to the kids, "He is much more, for better or worse, much more similar to the kids that we want to do better for than I was growing up, and I think that's a tremendous asset.... That's a set of experiences that I simply did not have that I think will help to make him especially impactful" (Camera, 1995).

King said that his goals for his time as secretary matched those of Duncan and President Obama. "There's a very clear agenda that Arne and the president have laid out over the last six and a half years that is right for the country." The agenda included continuing to push states to adopt higher standards, to ensure students are better prepared for college and careers, to expand access to early childhood education, and to expand access and improve completion of higher education.

"That agenda is very robust and I think I bring to it my experiences and my sense of urgency about kids who are most at risk, particularly because I see myself in them," King said. "These last 16 months will be an opportunity to build on the last six-and-a-half years" (Camera, 2015). King was a staunch supporter of the Common Core standards:

> The Common Core didn't invent good teaching, nor does it relieve us of the hard work of implementation. However, the Common Core is the first set of learning standards back-mapped grade by grade from what students need to know and be able to do in college and the workforce.... Data on the National Assessment of Educational Progress reveal that when states adopt rigorous learning standards and raise standards for teaching, significant gains in student performance follow. (Atkinson, 2015)

Due to this approach and his reputation as a "corporate educator," the appointment of King was opposed by the New York State United teachers' unions (Atkinson, 2015).

King was a strong supporter of classroom diversity (Atkinson, 2015). King stressed that racially and socioeconomically integrated classrooms provided better outcomes in students' academic performances and narrowed the achievement gap. While commissioner in New York, King announced a grant program that would give as much as $1.25 million to support socioeconomic integration programs in 25 of the state's low-performing schools.

IN THE NEWS 2016–2017

Obama provided funds for emergency water in Flint, Michigan. Russia and the US participated in Syrian peace talks. Supreme Court Justice Scalia died. There was an earthquake in Ecuador. Music legend Prince died. Obama visited Hiroshima. There was a shooting at a nightclub in Orlando, Florida. The United Kingdom voted for Brexit. Pokémon Go was a huge success. Mother Teresa was sainted and the world headed to the Olympics in Brazil.

Donald Trump beat Hillary Clinton for the presidency. Hurricane Matthew wreaked havoc in Haiti and in the southeastern US. Fidel Castro died. The Dakota Pipeline controversy continued. The Syrian government recaptured Aleppo.

King was secretary of education until Donald Trump was sworn in as president of the United States. Phil Rosenfelt stepped in and was acting secretary until Trump appointed Elizabeth "Betsy" DeVos.

Chapter 11

Elizabeth "Betsy" DeVos
2017–2021

To a casual observer, a classroom today looks scarcely different than what one looked like when I entered the public policy debate thirty years ago.

—Elizabeth DeVos

Republicans don't want to pay teachers enough. Democrats don't want to reform tenure laws. It's another partisan stand-off.

—Elizabeth DeVos

Too many students are up against another "empire"—governments, unions, associations of this, and organizations of that. It's an education cabal that protects the status quo at the expense of just about everyone else.

—Elizabeth DeVos

I fight against anyone who would have government be the parent to everyone.

—Elizabeth DeVos

In February 2017, Elizabeth "Betsy" DeVos was narrowly confirmed by a vote of 51–50 as the eleventh secretary of education. "All I ask for is an open mind and the opportunity to share my heart. . . . I've been involved in education issues for 28 years, as an activist, a citizen-volunteer and an advocate for children," said Devos (Philanthropy Roundtable, 2013).

The choice of DeVos was largely criticized by the education community due to her lack of public school credentials. Supporters believed that her lack of ties to the teachers' unions was an asset. In fact, the president of the American Federation of Teachers, Randi Weingarten, called DeVos the "the most anti-public education nominee who has ever been nominated for that position." Thus began the turbulent appointment of Betsy DeVos.

DeVos was born Elizabeth "Betsy" Prince on January 1958 in Holland, Michigan. She is described as a philanthropist and political activist (Bauer, n.d.). DeVos graduated from Calvin College with a degree in business economics. She married and became actively involved in politics with the Republican Party. She spent time volunteering and served on boards that support equity in education, school choice, and the arts.

DeVos had an early interest in education. Her interest began with her mother, who was a public school teacher. Secretary DeVos had been involved in education policy for nearly three decades as an advocate for children and a voice for parents when she was appointed. She is especially passionate about reforms that help underserved children gain access to a quality education (Bauer, n.d.). This interest increased when, as she had kids, she saw and realized the discrepancy between the quality of education her children were afforded versus those who were not as well off. DeVos mentored at-risk children for over twenty years.

> I got involved by starting a foundation that gave scholarships to low-income families so that parents could decide where their kids would go to school. We realized very quickly that, while it was wonderful to help some families through the scholarship fund, it was never going to fundamentally address the real problem. Most parents were not going to get the scholarship they wanted, and that meant most kids would not have the opportunities they deserved. (Philanthropy Roundtable, 2013)

DeVos's activity with the Republican Party and the subsequent donations to candidates and party activities became a major criticism about her and her appointment as secretary.

The goals that DeVos had for her time as secretary of education were straightforward. She said that education had been her passion "because of the public's awareness that traditional public schools are not succeeding. In fact, let's be clear, in many cases, they are failing. That's helped people become more open to what were once considered really radical reforms—reforms like vouchers, tax credits, and education savings accounts" (Gorman, 2017a).

DeVos was a vocal supporter of charter schools. "Charter schools are another choice—a very valid choice. As we work to help provide parents with more educational choices, it was always with the assumption that charter schools are part of the equation" (Gorman, 2017a). She proposed Education Freedom Scholarships which would follow students and allow them to choose schools that were "best for them."

While the proposal failed, she will be remembered "for leading the charge for every student's right to seek their best educational fit" (Turner, 2020). While an active champion, there is some concern that her involvement has actually hurt the choice movement more than it has helped it. DeVos and President Trump so polarized the issue that they may have sacrificed bipartisan support (Turner, 2020).

DeVos supported local control for schools. While she did not have a specific solution for the problems facing education, she knew what the answer would not be. "It won't be a giant bureaucracy or a federal department. Nope. The answer isn't bigger government. The answer is local control" (Philanthropy Roundtable, 2013).

DeVos was interested in reform at the postsecondary level. A press release from the Department of Education dated April 3, 2019, reported that the secretary's proposed "Accreditation and Innovation" higher education reforms reached consensus on the text of the draft rules. The package of higher education regulations was aimed at rethinking higher education to improve outcomes and accountability for students, institutions and taxpayers. "Today's historic action proves just how much can be accomplished on behalf of students when we put their needs above all else," said Secretary DeVos (U.S. Deptartment of Education, 2019).

"Rethinking higher education required each person at the negotiating table to challenge assumptions and examine past practice in order to better serve students. I commend them for doing just that" (U.S. Deptartment of Education, 2019).

DeVos worked to tighten the requirements for the students who were requesting repayment from for-profit colleges. Under the new guidelines, "Borrowers must prove they were misled and provide evidence of the school's intent to mislead them" (Turner, 2020). Upon learning that the TEACH grants—the grants that provided loan repayment for teachers willing to teach in underserved areas—were difficult and creating problems for the students due to difficult paperwork, she and her team apologized and worked to improve the process (Turner, 2020).

DeVos and President Trump worked together to reverse many of the decisions made by the Obama administration. As an example, in May 2016, the Obama administration provided a directive that allows a student to use the bathroom that matches their gender identity. In February 2017, Trump retracted the gender bathroom directive (Sass, 2022). They reversed an Obama era decision about racial discrimination in discipline, returning the control of discipline issues to the state and local governing bodies (Turner, 2020).

While DeVos was in office, other social issues took the national stage. During the 2018 and 2019 school years, teachers in many areas had teacher strikes, including Los Angeles and Chicago (Sass, 2022). While she had no role in negotiations, reports indicate that over 50% of the signs held by striking teachers were in opposition to Secretary DeVos (Turner, 2020).

IN THE NEWS

In the news during this time there were rallies and protests and weather events. There was the Women's March, the Unite the Right rally, the Charlotteville protests, the #MeToo movement, and football teams "taking a knee" (Brown, 2017). Hurricanes Irma, Henry, and Maria, and California wildfires reminded Americans that Mother Nature was a reckoning force. The US focused on gun violence following the shooting in Las Vegas, several school shootings, and the anniversary of the shooting at Columbine.

Internationally, things deteriorated further in Venezuela and Yemen, as well as in southern Africa. A Washington Post journalist was killed in a Saudi consulate in Istanbul. Great Britain left the European Union. Trump declared that North Korea was no longer a nuclear threat, as well as ended trade agreements and imposed large tariffs on big ticket international items, especially those from China.

The United States and China entered a trade war (Lindsay, 2018). The US leaves the Iran nuclear agreement (Lindsay, 2018). Brazil set the Amazon on fire and asylum seekers from Central America flood the US (Lindsay, 2018). Protestors took to the streets in Hong Kong and Iraq. The cathedral at Notre Dame burned. The year 2020 seemed to be the "worst" year anyone had seen in a long time. In January, the impeachment trial of Donald Trump began and Amy Coney Barrett was appointed and approved for the Supreme Court.

The first case of the coronavirus was documented and travel bans began (CNN, 2022). Jussie Smollett was indicted for a false hate crime. Harvey Weinstein was found guilty of sex crimes, as was Jeffery Epstein. A tornado hit Nashville. Trump declared a National Emergency in response to the coronavirus and the CDC began canceling events of more than 50 people. There were college admission scandals and subways closed across the US. George Floyd was murdered by Minneapolis police officers. Rayshard Brooks was shot.

The Supreme Court ruled that gay, lesbian, and transgender individuals are protected under civil rights laws. In Mississippi, the Confederate flag was removed from the state flag. John Lewis died. Kobe Bryant died. There was an earthquake in North Carolina. There were more shootings. There were Black Lives Matter protests. More Trump advisers were indicted. Trump was acquitted. There were hurricanes and more fires. Ruth Bader Ginsburg died and was the first woman to lie in state at the U.S. Capitol.

Drug companies released vaccines. Biden was declared the winner of the 2020 presidential election. Worldwide there were hurricanes and avalanches and more fires. Fires rolled across Australia. This list is not inclusive but does demonstrate that the early decades of the new century took on a flavor all its own. In this, Elizabeth DeVos tried to make sense of school choice and rereleased the Career and Technical Education Act.

DeVos took a narrow view of Title IX rulings. In her interpretations, she gave more rights to the accused. The department changed the definition of sexual harassment under Title IX to mean something that was "severe, pervasive and objectively offensive." While these changes met with some opposition, overall DeVos and her team is credited with coming "up with a Title IX playbook [that is fair]" (Turner, 2020). Under her guidance, the department suspended student loan repayments and had zero percent interest rates during the COVID-19 shutdowns (Turner, 2020). While she had many critics, including the teachers' unions, she did manage to accomplish some of her goals.

In February 2019, Secretary of Education Elizabeth "Betsy" DeVos donated a large portion of her salary to the Thurgood Marshall College Fund and other philanthropic organizations. In March 2019, DeVos worked with President Trump to create "Freedom of Speech" legislation for college campuses. In this legislation, federal funding would be tied to guarantees that postsecondary institutions would support and not suppress free speech on their campuses.

One of the most controversial proposals DeVos made was to cut funding for the Special Olympics (Binkley, 2019). Her rationalization was that while she personally supports and is in favor of the organization, it raises $100 million annually and the $7 million she proposed to cut could be used in other places.

DeVos was secretary of education from 2017 until she submitted her resignation January 7, 2021. She stated that the president's behavior regarding the January 6 insurrection was the reason for her resignation. Secretary DeVos had been involved in education policy for nearly three decades as an advocate for children and a voice for parents. While much of what she did as secretary was to undo what had been done, "Perhaps her most remarkable achievement wasn't in the realm of policy at all, but in the fact that she became a household name—as a *Cabinet secretary*—and brought a white-hot spotlight to the debate about how America should educate its children" (Turner, 2020).

Chapter 12
Miguel Cardona
2021–present

We need to focus on not only recovering from the pandemic but also look towards our students' education after the pandemic to ensure there are improved resources to build our education system back better than before. This budget ensures all students have access to high-quality, affordable postsecondary education, while also improving career pathways for students of all ages and levels.

—Miguel Cardona

There is a saying in Spanish: En la unión está la fuerza. In unity there is strength.

—Miguel Cardona

On March 1, 2021, the Senate confirmed Miguel Cardona as the twelfth U.S. secretary of education. Cardona was approved by a 64–33 vote, placing the former Connecticut education commissioner in charge of a $102+ billion department with 4,400 employees. Before being nominated by President Biden, Cardona served as Connecticut's education commissioner. Miguel Cardona spent a year and a half arguing forcefully that schools should reopen during the COVID-19 crisis in order to keep equity gaps from growing ever wider (Turner, 2021).

Miguel Cardona was born in Meriden, Connecticut. He grew up in public housing and learned English as a second language (Blad & Ujifusa, 2021). Cardona graduated from high school and received an undergraduate degree in bilingual education from Central Connecticut University. He became Connecticut's youngest principal at the age of 28. In 2012, he was awarded the National Distinguished Principal Award for Connecticut (Education Week Library Staff, 2021b). Cardona earned both his master's degree and doctorate from the University of Connecticut. In 2019, he became the superintendent for the State of Connecticut (U.S. Department of Education, 2021a).

In his early career, Cardona focused on early education for three- to five-year-old children. Under Cardona's leadership, Connecticut launched a statewide FAFSA Data Dashboard, procured a comprehensive statewide Special Education Data System (CT-SEDS), and announced the state's highest ever extended graduation rates for students with disabilities and English learners (Blad & Ujifusa, 2021).

According to National Public Radio's *All Things Considered*, "[T]he stakes are, perhaps, higher than they have ever been for a [potential] secretary of education" (Turner & Uzunlar, 2021). During his confirmation hearing in February 2021, Cardona echoed the Biden administration's position, saying, "[I]f we don't assess where our students are and their level of performance, it's going to be difficult for us to provide targeted support and resource allocation in the manner that can best support the closing of the gaps that have been exacerbated due to this pandemic" (Turner, 2021).

That may or may not be true. Of the issues at hand, Cardona needs to mitigate and manage the safe return to schools and significant changes related to the pandemic, including testing, learning loss, and being able to keep schools open (Carlton, 2021; Turner & Uzunlar, 2021). Additionally, Cardona must address the dire federal student aid program and the role of the Department of Education in enforcement for programs and accountability (Carlton, 2021). When asked about the student loan forgiveness plan, Cardona stated that he would like to work with Congress on this issue, although the Biden administration suggested that they would work unilaterally through the Department of Education.

In October 2021, President Biden released the Build Back Better framework which outlined a three-part plan to subsidize communities with $3.5 trillion for economic recovery following the COVID-19 outbreak. While the measure passed the House of Representatives (220–207) it stalled in the Senate, where it was "slimmed down" and revitalized as the Inflation Reduction Act of 2022 (Smith, 2022). The bill, which authorized $737 billion in spending, passed with no Republican support.

The president signed the bill into law August 16, 2022. Cardona supported the bill and stressed that it will be good for the American people and that it will help those from disadvantaged backgrounds, calling "naysayers unAmerican" (Treon, 2022). He supports the universal preschool, increased financial support of childcare, promise of free community college, and student loan forgiveness proposed in the plan.

Under the new Biden Inflation Reduction Act (IRA), adults making up to $125,000 may qualify for student loan forgiveness up to $20,000 and may see a 20-year cap on student loan repayment. While there has been a lot of controversy on this issue, Cardona believes it is legal for the Department of Education to pay off student loans as it is stated in the Heroes Act, page 637. The Heroes Act gives the authority to provide a waiver to ensure that Americans are not worse off after an emergency—a national emergency, which the pandemic was (Stone, 2022).

In light of the pandemic and the highlighted learning disparities, Cardona needs to, just as every secretary of education has, address school choice (Turner & Uzunlar, 2021). School choice was a topic that was strongly supported by the previous education secretary. When asked about school choice, he responded, "My passion really is to ensure quality schools, period. . . . Making sure that we're not supporting a system of winners and losers where, if you get into a school, you have an opportunity for success, but if you don't get into a school, your options lead to at least a belief that you can't make it" (Turner & Uzunlar, 2021). He also stated that he believed that parents would rather send their kids to neighborhood schools and he would like to make sure those schools were all high caliber.

Cardona also intends "to rethink how we're [serving English language learners], and understand the value and benefit of not only being bilingual in this country, but being bicultural" (Menas, 2021). Pandemic has exacerbated inequalities. Parents of students with disabilities have voiced concerns about quality and consistency and question if schools are abiding by federal education law. On another issue that has played back and forth between administrations, when asked about the transgender athletic participation and the recent ruling under Title IX, Cardona said. "It's non-negotiable to make sure that our learning environments are places that are free of discrimination and harassment for all learners" (Menas, 2021).

Cardona needs to continue to differentiate himself from Elizabeth DeVos by providing more technical support and also by changing the tone of conversation from the department. He will try to give more public speeches and have more private conversations (Blad & Ujifusa, 2021). Cardona will also continue to work to create distance between himself and the last Democratic administration, as they had a different focus.

Obama created controversy on charter schools, accountability, and testing but those will not be front-burner issues. Cardona will continue to move the other direction. He will look to reinstate guidance on racial disparities and transgender issues. Biden has made it clear he wants these supported, just like he wants a more centralized approach to education (Blad & Ujifusa, 2021). Similar to Obama, Biden intends to prioritize grants. This directly impacts Cardona. While Cardona does not appropriate money, as that is this job of

Congress, he does oversee grant allocation. Now that pandemic concerns have started to wane, Cardona is facing increased pleas for help with academic recovery efforts; advice for dealing with emotionally charged public debates over the discussion of race, gender, and sexuality in classrooms; and ideas for addressing local teacher shortages (Stafford, 2022).

One of the most pressing issues remains a nationwide teacher shortage. In an article for *Education Week*, Cardona addresses this and points to the America Rescue Plan, that may bring 250,000 tutors into schools.

> Well, you know, state and local governments are the ones that move forward their assessment systems. What we're doing is providing support, accountability, and technical assistance to make sure that they're assessing where their students are and providing tutoring and afterschool programming to catch these students up. That's why the American Rescue Plan dollars made so much sense, and that's why across the country all states are benefiting from it. (Stone, 2022)

State legislatures have been very active since Cardona took office. In 2021 most press focused on COVID-19 and the responses of schools and teachers to the pandemic. In 2022, issues of race and sexuality seem to gain the most attention from the media. Several states outlawed the teaching of critical race theory and dictate how conversations about race are held. Similarly, Florida and Alabama passed laws prohibiting the teaching of content regarding sexual preference to students in younger grades (Sass, 2022). In May 2022, a school shooting in Texas brought the topic of guns and safety in schools back into the national headlines.

People who have worked with Cardona in the past say that he focuses on partnerships and listening. He supports autonomy for schools and within districts, as he demonstrated during the 2020 COVID-19 issues (Blad & Ujifusa, 2021). Secretary Cardona's approach to leadership in Connecticut focused on partnerships: within his Education Department; between state agencies; and with local boards, educator unions, school administrator associations, child advocates, and most importantly, students and families. By all appearances, he is continuing to try and do the same at the federal level.

IN THE NEWS

Race, gender equity, school choice, and gun control were all hot topics in the news in 2022. Additional conversation in schools was heard discussing the June 2022 Supreme Court decision on *Roe v. Wade*, which overturned abortion as a constitutional right and relegated it to the jurisdiction of the states. Trump was acquitted for inciting a riot with regard to the January 6 insurrection at the White House and his accusation of the Democrats "stealing" elections is still under review in some states (CBS News, 2021).

A container ship blocked the Suez Canal for six days. Derek Chauvin was convicted of the murder of George Floyd. Elon Musk sent a shuttle to space through a private company and a building in Florida collapsed. The US won 113 gold medals in the Olympics and Simone Biles called attention to the mental health of athletes. In August 2021, the United States pulled troops out of Afghanistan, which then fell within 11 days (CBS News, 2021).

The World Health Organization announced a malaria vaccine. Tornadoes ravaged the South and Midwest and the FDA gave emergency approval to an antiviral pill to treat COVID-19. The year 2022 was plagued by political and racial tensions and distrust of the government. The secretary of education will have to work hard to convince the American people that he is on their side and doing what is best for students.

Chapter 13

The Acting Secretaries

Ted Sanders (1990–1991), Phil Rosenfelt (January–February 2017 and January–March 2021), and Mick Zais (January 2021)

Since the Department of Education began in 1979, there have been three men who have acted as the secretary of education. These men have served while waiting for a candidate to be confirmed as Ted Sanders or Phil Rosenfelt did, or while a candidate was getting settled into office as Mick Zais did in 2021. It is interesting to look at the men who have stepped up and stepped in so a cabinet seat was not vacant.

The Federal Vacancies Reform Act (FVRA) allows that certain jobs, especially those which require Senate approval, may be filled on an acting basis, in order to ensure there is someone in place to carry out the duties of the position until someone is approved by the Senate. Theoretically, at least, the law limits the amount of time an acting secretary can serve, restricts the "acting" designation to someone with experience in the department in question, and gives the Senate the ability to enforce the law (Caba, 2019).

TED SANDERS

John Theodore "Ted" Sanders was acting secretary of education from 1990 until 1991 under President George H. W. Bush. Sanders was born on September 19, 1941, in Littlefield, Texas. Both of his parents had college degrees and Sanders was the oldest of three sons. Ted graduated from high school and earned a bachelor's degree in mathematics. His first foray into education was as a math teacher in the state of Idaho.

Sanders continued to teach, including teaching second grade with the Bureau of Indian Affairs in New Mexico. He received a master' degree in mathematics from Washington State University and a doctorate from the University of Nevada. Following his master's work, he went on to work for the New Mexico Department of Education. From his position within the department in New Mexico, Ted was hired as superintendent for the state of Nevada.

In 1985, Sanders was recruited and hired as state superintendent for the Illinois State Board of Education. He remained in Illinois until he was invited to Washington, DC, by President George H. W. Bush to serve as deputy secretary of education (Hecht, 2015). Sanders initially declined the position, but he was eventually persuaded. As deputy secretary, he was asked to serve as interim secretary upon Cavazos's resignation. He returned to the deputy secretary position under Lamar Alexander and served the U.S. Department of Education until 1991, when he was named Ohio state superintendent of public instruction (Hecht, 1995).

PHIL ROSENFELT

Phillip "Phil" Rosenfelt is a career employee within the Department of Education (Suglia, 2017). Before agreeing to accept the role as interim secretary of education, Rosenfelt was the deputy general counsel for Program Service in the Office of General Counsel at the Education Department, where he had served for 10 years (Browne & Payson-Denney, 2017). Rosenfelt was chosen by outgoing Secretary John King. Rosenfelt was described as a "trusted hard worker with 'encyclopedic knowledge' of the Department of Education" (Suglia, 2017).

Phil Rosenfelt was born in New Jersey. He received a bachelor of science degree from the University of Pennsylvania and a law degree from Columbia University. Rosenfelt got an additional LLM or master of laws from New York University. Rosenfelt worked for the Department of Education since its creation, starting off his career in government in 1971 at the Department of Health, Education, and Welfare. Later the Department of Education would become a separate department (Nicosia, 2017).

Before becoming acting secretary, Rosenfelt oversaw legal services for the Department of Education, regarding the development and implementation of federal programs (Suglia, 2017). Earlier in his career, he was also responsible for the desegregation of a school in Alabama and ensuring all students had education in the United States, regardless of their immigration status (Suglia, 2017). Rosenfelt was part of a guidance released to schools to ensure that all students have access to education regardless of immigration status (Gorman, 2017b).

Following the failure of No Child Left Behind (NCLB) reauthorization, Rosenfelt helped update requirements so states could still be held accountable for providing quality education to students without being held to the outdated requirements of NCLB. "It was a very open and collaborative kind of discussion where we were also looking at information we had on how well the programs were working—which provisions seemed to be working and which did not" (Gorman, 2017b).

In 2013, Rosenfelt was an honoree for what is fondly nicknamed "The Sammies," or the Oscars of government service. Rosenfelt was honored for using his legal expertise to better education in the United States through his position at the Department of Education (Gorman, 2017b). In his spare time, Rosenfelt likes baseball and rock and roll. He has found time to be a rock music critic, teach education law, and practice stand-up comedy (Nicosia, 2017).

Rosenfelt was a good interim choice because he knows, regardless of politics, how to keep things moving. "The [career staffers] know how to do all the things that are needed," said Peter Cunningham, who oversaw communications under Secretary of Education Arne Duncan. "The actual day-to-day work, of putting out money and reviewing accountability proposals and plans, engaging with the states and districts for whatever reason, all that stuff continues. What does stop in the wake of the new administration is policy making" (Nicosia, 2017).

MICK ZAIS

Mitchell "Mick" McGeever Zais was born December 10, 1946, in Fort Bragg, North Carolina. Mick earned a bachelor of science degree in engineering from West Point, a master's and doctorate in social psychology and organizational behavior from the University of Washington, a master of arts in military history from the School for Advanced Military Studies at Fort Leavenworth, Kansas, and did postdoctoral studies in National Security Affairs at the National Defense University in Washington, DC (Zais, 2018).

Zais served as deputy secretary of the U.S. Department of Education. He was confirmed by the U.S. Senate on May 16, 2018, after being nominated by President Donald J. Trump on October 5, 2017. Zais was confirmed by a vote of 50–48. As deputy secretary, he stepped in as secretary of education following the resignation of Elizabeth DeVos.

He retired from the military as a brigadier general after 31 years of active duty. Following his retirement, he became president of Newberry College, to much acclaim. Zais was actively involved in accreditation and postsecondary organizations while president at Newberry. After 10 years at Newberry, Zais was elected to the role of superintendent of the South Carolina Department of Education. His combination of exceptional military and education service made him a good candidate to act as secretary while waiting for the swearing in of President Biden's secretary of education, Miguel Cardona.

Conclusion

The United States has had 13 secretaries of education. There have been three women, two secretaries were Latinx, and two were African American. Five have been registered Democrats. Eight have been registered Republicans; two of those eight started out as registered Democrats. Some of the secretaries came from humble backgrounds; while others came from advantaged backgrounds. One secretary was a billionaire who only took a $1 salary. This is a relatively diverse group of individuals, but they all demonstrated that they had one thing in common. Each of the secretaries of education believed that education is the great equalizer. Whether they were deemed effective or not, what each secretary said publicly was that it is important to make sure American children are achieving, as defined by obtaining academic goals, and that all U.S. children are achieving—not just a select few.

At a gathering of the living U.S. secretaries of education at Duke University in 2002, while there was not consensus about standardized testing or how to close the achievement gap, there was agreement that "the role of the U.S. Department of Education is to shape broad values and policies, to rally support for them, and to bring a national commitment to serving the underserved" (Dodge, 2002). It seems that all the secretaries believed there should be a Department of Education, whether they came in believing it or not.

An interesting exercise to do with students of all ages is to present them with a table that breaks down and categorizes the signers of the Declaration of Independence. Students are then tasked with asking questions based on the information that was presented. When they look at the information, what questions arise? This small critical thinking exercise (from an unknown source) encourages students to draw information out and ask questions based on perceived patterns and only on what they have in front of them.

There is a similar table in the appendix as a summary of the information within this book. The table includes the name and the age of each secretary when they were sworn in to office, the years served, his or her political affiliation, home state, education, professional background, the budget of the department, and the acts passed during each appointment. This is just as a matter of interest. Do with the information what you will.

The purpose of gathering information is so that it can be examined. Look for patterns. Ask questions. Here are some examples:

- Why, if Republicans are so concerned with government overreach, has the budget increased most under Republican presidents?
- What role, if any, does an advanced degree have in being a good secretary of education? Three of the secretaries stopped with bachelor degrees. Did that impact them positively or negatively?
- How can it be that the same three questions have been asked in the tenure of every secretary?
- What is the role of the federal government in education?
- How do we close achievement gaps?
- Should we allow, is it more equitable to permit school choice?

These are just a few of the questions that come to mind with all the information gathered in one place. As different groups of students and constituents view this table, there will be new and different questions. Hopefully.

When cabinet secretaries leave office, they get to take their chairs with them (Parker, 1978). They actually take the physical chair—the one they sat in while they worked. Of the thirteen secretaries of education to date, twelve have taken their chairs. As future secretaries move in and out of the office, it will be interesting to see how they add data to this table and what perspectives they bring to the questions that have been asked since the inception of the department. Keep examining information. Keep asking questions.

Appendix
The U.S. Secretaries of Education, 1979–present

Name	Age	Dates	President	Party	Home state	Highest Degree	Profession	Starting Dept. budget (in billions)	Acts passed/ Important facts
Miguel Cardona	47	3/21-present	Biden	D	CT	EdD	Educator	95	Inflation Reduction Act 2022 Student Loan Forgiveness
Mitchell Zais		1/21-3/21	Trump	D	SC	MA	Education/ military	-	Acting Sec.
Elizabeth DeVos	63	2017-2021	Trump	R	MI	BA	Philanthropist	115	2018/2019-teacher strikes! 18 school shootings in 2018 April 20, 2018 National Walk Out Day-students walk out in protest of gun violence March 2020 World Health Organization declares COVID-19 pandemic Strengthening Career and Technical Education for the 21st Century Act (reauthorization 2006 Perkins IV
Phil Rosenfelt		1/17-2/17 & 1/21-3/21	Trump Biden	I	NJ	JD	Legal counsel Dept of Ed	-	Acting Sec. (2X)
John King, Jr.	42	2016-2017	Obama	R	NY	JD/EdD	Education	77	Common Core Standards
Arne Duncan	52	2009-2016	Obama	D	IL	Bachelor/ honorary doctorate	Private Ed.	39-Appropriated, 98-Recovery Act	ARRA Race to the Top Common Core launched 2013 virtual schools in 25 states ESSA (Every Student Succeeds Act) replaces NCLB
Margaret Spellings	52	2005-2009	Bush	R	TX	Bachelor	Education/ Politics	71	Implemented NCLB Plan for Higher Education
Rod Paige	72	2001-2005	Bush	R	MS/IN/FL/TX	EdD	Education	42	Passed NCLB Uncovered fraud in department & reworked management structure
Richard Riley	68	1993-2001	Clinton	D	SC	JD	Politics	32	1994 First online high school opens Goals 2000
Lamar Alexander	53	1991-1993	Bush	R	TN	JD	Politics-Senator	28	America 2000 First charter school opens 1992, MN
Ted Sanders		1990-1991	Bush	R	IL	EdD	Education/ Higher Ed	-	Acting Sec. IDEA passes
Lauro Cavazos	63	1988-1990	Bush	D	TX	PhD	Higher Ed	20	NGA's 6 goals and created new federal student aid regulations
William Bennett	45	1985-1988	Reagan	D/R	NC	PhD/JD	Education/ Politics	18	Reauthorized ESEA
Terrel Bell	63	1981-1984	Reagan	R	UT	PhD	Education		'Nation At Risk' Inspired the Terrel Bell Award for Distinguished Principals
Shirley Hufstedler	57	1979-1981	Carter	D	CA	LLB-Bachelor of Law	Law/Judiciary	14	Started Department- moved 160 programs into one area

Fig. 0.A

References

Adams, J. E., Jr. (n.d.). Education reform: Overview, reports of historical significance. Retrieved August 24, 2022, from https://education.stateuniversity.com/pages/1944/Education-Reform.html

American Institute of Physics. (2008). President Bush signals his intention for American competitiveness initiative. AIG.org. Retrieved December 1, 2022, from https://www.aip.org/fyi/2008/president-bush-signals-his-intention-american-competitiveness-initiative

Associated Press. (1979, September 28). Department of Education approved by House. *Pittsburgh Post-Gazette*, via Google News. Retrieved August 14, 2022, from https://news.google.com/newspapers?id=_J5RAAAAIBAJ&sjid=6W0DAAAAIBAJ&pg=2930,4340566&dq=department-of-education&hl=en

Associated Press. (2004, November 12). Education secretary Paige reportedly to resign: Education Secretary Rod Paige intends to leave his Cabinet post, an administration official said Friday. NBC News. Retrieved August 26, 2022, from https://www.nbcnews.com/id/wbna6471630

Associated Press (2022, March 18). Lauro Cavazos, first Latino Cabinet member, dies at 95. Retrieved August 26, 2022, from https://www.nbcnews.com/news/latino/lauro-cavazos-first-latino-cabinet-member-dies-95-rcna20709

Atkinson, K. (2015, October 3). Three facts about John King, the next education secretary. MSNBC. Retrieved August 18, 2022, from https://www.msnbc.com/msnbc/what-we-know-about-john-king-the-next-education-secretary-msna695821

Bauer, P. (n.d.). Betsy DeVos: American stateswoman. In Britannica. Retrieved August 23, 2022, from https://www.britannica.com/biography/Betsy-DeVos

Bell, T. H. (1988). *The thirteenth man: A Reagan cabinet memoir*. The Free Press, A Division of Macmillan, Inc.

Bell, T. H., & Elmquist, D. L. (1992). An appraisal of secretary of education Lamar Alexander's first year in office. *Phi Delta Kappan, 73*(10), 757–759.

Bennett, W. (1988). C-SPAN interview. Retrieved https://www.c-span.org/video/?5719-1/interview-william-bennett

Binkley, C. (2019). DeVos defends plan to eliminate Special Olympics funding. ABC News. Retrieved August 31, 2022, from https://abc3340.com/news/nation-world/devos-defends-plan-to-eliminate-special-olympics-funding

Blad, E., & Ujifusa, A. (2021, January 5). 5 things to know about Dr. Miguel Cardona: Biden's choice for ed. secretary. *Education Week*. Retrieved August 30, 2022, from https://www.edweek.org/policy-politics/video-5-things-to-know-about-dr-miguel-cardona-bidens-choice-for-ed-secretary/2021/01

Bowen, E. (1985, May 20). Education: The secretary of controversy: William Bennett. *Time*. Retrieved August 25, 2022, from https://content.time.com/time/subscriber/printout/0,8816,956353,00.html

Brown, T. B. (2017, December 28). Some of 2017's biggest national stories, in pictures. National Public Radio. Retrieved August 31, 2022, from https://www.npr.org/2017/12/28/572110710/some-of-2017s-biggest-national-stories-in-pictures

Browne, R., & Payson-Denney, W. (2017, January 19). The people you don't know who could be running the government on Friday. CNN. Retrieved August 30, 2022, from https://www.cnn.com/2017/01/18/politics/temporary-cabinet-trump/

Bush, G. H. W. (1991). Remarks at the swearing in for Lamar Alexander as secretary of education. The American Presidency. Retrieved August 29, 2022, from https://www.presidency.ucsb.edu/documents/remarks-the-swearing-ceremony-for-lamar-alexander-secretary-education

Bush, G. W. (2001). September 11, 2001: Attack on America remarks by the president after two planes crash into the world trade center. Remarks office of the press secretary. Retrieved July 28, 2022, from https://avalon.law.yale.edu/sept11/president_008.asp

Caba, S. (2019). It's complicated: "Acting" cabinet secretaries raise questions of accountability. *American Insight*. Retrieved August 30, 2022, from https://freespeechblog.org/its-complicated-acting-cabinet-secretaries-raise-questions-of-accountability/

Camera, L. (2015, October 20). What John King has that Arne Duncan doesn't: Incoming education secretary John King's past could make him especially effective. *U.S. News*. Retrieved July 30, 2022, from https://www.usnews.com/news/articles/2015/10/20/what-john-kings-brings-to-the-education-department

Carlton, G. (2021). In March 2021, the senate confirmed Miguel Cardona as the U.S. secretary of education. *What Does the Secretary of Education Actually Do?* Retrieved August 10, 2022, from https://thebestschools.org/magazine/what-does-secretary-of-education-do/ (site discontinued)

CBS News. (2004, November 4). Bush education secretary to resign. CBS News. Retrieved September 14, 2022, from https://www.cbsnews.com/news/bush-education-secretary-to-resign/

CBS News. (2021). The year in review: Top news stories of 2021 month-by-month. CBS News. Retrieved August 28, 2022, from https://www.cbsnews.com/news/the-year-in-review-top-news-stories-of-2021-month-by-month/

Center for Education Policy (CEP). (2020). *History and evolution of public education in the U.S.* The George Washington University Graduate School of Education & Human Development. Retrieved August 8, 2022, from https://files.eric.ed.gov/fulltext/ED606970.pdf

Chapell, B. (2020, March 11). Coronavirus: COVID-19 is now officially a pandemic, WHO says. National Public Radio. Retrieved August 31, 2022, from https://www

.npr.org/sections/goatsandsoda/2020/03/11/814474930/coronavirus-covid-19-is-now-officially-a-pandemic-who-says

Chebatoris, J. (2012). The talented Mr. Riley: Richard W. Riley has a knack for being chosen. Retrieved August 31, 2022, from https://www.furman.edu/wp-content/uploads/sites/195/rileypdfFiles/RileyArticle10.31.12MrTalentedTownMag.pdf.pdf

CNN. (2022, February 2). 2020 in review fast facts. CNN. Retrieved August 30, 2022, from https://edition.cnn.com/2020/12/10/us/2020-in-review-fast-facts/index.html

Clarke, S. (2016). The top news stories of 2016: Look back through the most noteworthy stories of the year. *U.S. News & World Report*. Retrieved August 31, 2022, from https://www.usnews.com/news/national-news/slideshows/top-news-stories-of-2016

Congressional Research Service (CRS). (2019). Record number R45827. Retrieved June 22, 2023, from https://sgp.fas.org/crs/misc/R45827.pdf

Congress of the U.S. (1995). Goals 2000. Hearing before a Subcommittee of the Committee on Appropriations, United States Senate. One Hundred Fourth Congress, First Session. Special Hearing. Retrieved August 26, 2022, from https://eric.ed.gov/?id=ED400595

Cooper, K. J., & Devroy, A. (1990, December 13). Cavazos out as education secretary. *Washington Post*. Retrieved August 23, 2022, from https://www.washingtonpost.com/archive/politics/1990/12/13/cavazos-out-as-education-secretary/a0a3214a-ab60-4938-8263-34c6e632fa3b/

Cross, C. T. (2010). *Political education: National policy comes of age. The updated edition*. Teachers College Press.

DeLoughry, T. J. (1990, December 19). White House reportedly asked Cavazos to resign. *The Chronicle of Higher Education*. Retrieved November 24, 2022, from https://www.chronicle.com/article/white-house-reportedly-asked-cavazos-to-resign/?cid=gen_sign_in

Dodge, K. A. (2002). Coming of age: The Department of Education. *Phi Delta Kappan*, 83(9), 671. Retrieved from https://eric.ed.gov/?id=EJ644964

DuBose, B. (2008, April 23). Education Secretary Margaret Spellings proposes revisions to No Child Left Behind Act. *Los Angeles Times*. Retrieved August 4, 2022, from https://www.csun.edu/pubrels/clips/April08/04-23-08R.pdf

Duncan, A. (2018). *How schools work: An inside account of failure and success from one of the nation's longest serving secretaries of education*. Simon & Schuster.

Education Trust. (2022). John B. King Jr., president. Retrieved August 27, 2022, from https://edtrust.org/team/john-b-king-jr/

Education Week. (n.d.). Lamar Alexander. *Education Week*. Retrieved August 31, 2022, from https://www.edweek.org/lamar-alexander

Education Week Library Staff. (2017a, August 18). At a glance: U.S. secretaries of education. *Education Week*. Retrieved from https://www.edweek.org/federal/at-a-glance-u-s-secretaries-of-education

Education Week Library Staff. (2017b, August 18). Lamar Alexander, fifth U.S. education secretary: Biography and achievements. *Education Week*. Retrieved August 23, 2022, from https://www.edweek.org/policy-politics/william-j-bennett-third-u-s-education-secretary-biography-and-acheivements/2017/08

Education Week Library Staff. (2017c, August 18). Richard W. Riley, sixth U.S. education secretary: Biography and achievements. *Education Week*. Retrieved July 30, 2022, from https://www.edweek.org/policy-politics/richard-w-riley-sixth-u-s-education-secretary-biography-and-achievements/2017/08

Education Week Library Staff. (2017d, August 18). Shirley Hufstedler, first U.S. education secretary: Biography and achievements. *Education Week*. Retrieved July 30, 2022, from https://www.edweek.org/policy-politics/shirley-hufstedler-first-u-s-education-secretary-biography-and-acheivements/2017/08

Education Week Library Staff. (2017e, August 18). William J. Bennett, third U.S. education secretary: Biography and achievements. *Education Week*. Retrieved August 23, 2022, from https://www.edweek.org/policy-politics/william-j-bennett-third-u-s-education-secretary-biography-and-acheivements/2017/08

Education Week Library Staff. (2021a, March 1). At a glance: U.S. secretaries of education. *Education Week*. Retrieved from https://www.edweek.org/federal/at-a-glance-u-s-secretaries-of-education

Education Week Library Staff. (2021b, March 1). Miguel Cardona, U.S. secretary of education: Background and achievements. *Education Week*. Retrieved August 30, 2022, from https://www.edweek.org/policy-politics/miguel-cardona-u-s-secretary-of-education-background-and-achievements/2021/03

Education Week Library Staff. (2022, March 25). Lauro F. Cavazos, fourth U.S. education secretary: Biography and achievements. *Education Week*. Retrieved August 28, 2022, from https://www.edweek.org/policy-politics/lauro-f-cavazos-fourth-u-s-education-secretary-biography-and-achievements/2017/08

Elam, S. (1981). The National Education Association: Political powerhouse or paper tiger? *Phi Delta Kappan, 63*(3), 169–174.

Emma, C., Ciaramella, A. G., & Hefling, K. (2015, October 2). Education Secretary Duncan stepped down. *Politico*. Retrieved July 20, 2022, from https://www.politico.com/story/2015/10/education-secretary-arne-duncan-is-stepping-down-in-december-214374

Encyclopedia.com. (2018a). Margaret Spellings. *Encyclopedia of World Biography*. Retrieved from https://www.notablebiographies.com/newsmakers2/2005-Pu-Z/Spellings-Margaret.html

Encyclopedia.com. (2018b). William John Bennett. *Encyclopedia of World Biography*. Retrieved from https://www.encyclopedia.com/people/history/historians-miscellaneous-biographies/william-j-bennett

Encyclopedia.com. (2019). Retrieved June 22, 2023, from https://www.encyclopedia.com/history/encyclopedias-almanacs-transcripts-and-maps/cavazos-lauro

Epstein, N., & Lescaze, L. (1981, January 7). Terrel Bell reported choice to become education secretary. *Washington Post*. Retrieved August 21, 2022, from https://www.washingtonpost.com/archive/politics/1981/01/07/terrel-bell-reported-choice-to-become-education-secretary/c6fcb831-6971-498d-b1e0-8517a8d0cd03/

Events History. (2014). Years 1979–2014. Retrieved from http://www.eventshistory.com

Finn, C. E., Jr. (2022). Leadership makes a difference: Lamar Alexander and K–12 education: As governor, secretary of education, and senator, Alexander had vast influence. *Education Next*, 22(3). Retrieved August 28, 2022, from https://docs.google.com/document/d/10w_Hw1QXZoXs7jN5DC0xTS7afwRs-aEm3FAta6dmu08/edit#

Fox, T. (2011, July 21). Richard Riley, former U.S. secretary of education, on his leadership lessons. *Washington Post*. Retrieved June 20, 2023, from https://www.washingtonpost.com/blogs/ask-the-fedcoach/post/richard-riley-former-us-secretary-of-education-on-his-leadership-lessons/2011/03/04/gIQA0kDKSI_blog.html

Gaille, B. (2017, March 31). 34 spectacular William Bennett quotes. Retrieved August 30, 2022, from https://brandongaille.com/34-spectacular-william-bennett-quotes/

George W. Bush Presidential Center. (2022). Margaret Spellings. Retrieved from https://www.bushcenter.org/people/margaret-spellings.html

Ginsburg, R. B. (2017). In memory of Shirley Mount Hufstedler. *Stanford Law Review*, 69(3), 603+. Retrieved from https://www.stanfordlawreview.org/print/article/in-memory-of-shirley-mount-hufstedler/

Gorman, N. (2017a, January 6). The top 10 Betsy DeVos Quotes that explain her goals as secretary of education. *Education World*. Retrieved August 25, 2022, from https://www.educationworld.com/a_news/top-10-betsy-devos-quotes-education-explain-her-goals-secretary-education-2126212998

Gorman, N. (2017b, February 1). Who's in charge right now? 5 facts to know about acting education secretary Philip Rosenfelt. *Education World*. Retrieved August 20, 2022, from: https://www.educationworld.com/a_news/who's-charge-right-now-5-facts-know-about-acting-education-secretary-philip-rosenfelt

Gross, G. (2012, November 27). Dr. Gail Gross interviews Bill Bennett. Retrieved August 30, 2022, from https://www.youtube.com/watch?v=b4hvAkd4UfU&t=154s

Grosvenor, C. R., Jr. (2016). Inthe80s [opensource]. Retrieved August 26, 2022, from http://www.inthe80s.com

Hanushek, E. A, Peterson, P. E., & Woessmann, L. (2014). U.S. students from educated families lag in international tests. *Education Next*, 14(4).

Hecht, A. (2015). States' impact on federal education policy oral history project. Ted Sanders: A narrative biographical summary. New York State Archives. Retrieved August 30, 2022, from https://www.nysarchivestrust.org/application/files/4415/7600/9415/Sanders.Bio.pdf

The high price of cheapening the cabinet. (1978, January 16). *New York Times*. Retrieved August 9, 2022, from https://www.nytimes.com/1978/01/16/archives/the-high-price-of-cheapening-the-cabinet.html

Hoffman, D., & Broder, D. S. (1989, September 29). Summit sets 7 main goals for education. *Washington Post*. Retrieved August 28, 2022, from https://www.washingtonpost.com/archive/politics/1989/09/29/summit-sets-7-main-goals-for-education/a0c8a8a4-d58a-4036-9b4a-e5cebeebab40/

Hufstedler, S. M. (1981, January 11). Open letter to a cabinet member. *New York Times Magazine*. Retrieved August 1, 2022, from https://nyti.ms/29KPpEg

Hufstedler, S. M. (2007, October 21). Oral interviews. C-SPAN. Retrieved July 30, 2022, from https://www.c-span.org/video/?316892-1/shirley-mount-hufstedler-oral-history-interview

Infoplease. (2017). Retrieved from https://www.infoplease.com/sources
Jefferson, T. (1779). A bill for the more general diffusion of knowledge. *The Jefferson Papers.* Retrieved August 8, 2022, from https://founders.archives.gov/documents/Jefferson/01-02-02-0132-0004-0079.
Jefferson, T. (1786). From Thomas Jefferson to George Wythe, 13 August 1786. Founders Online. Retrieved August 12, 2022, from https://founders.archives.gov/documents/Jefferson/01-10-02-0162.
Kaplan, L. S., & Owings, W. A. (2018). Betsy DeVos's education reform agenda: What principals—and their publics—need to know. *NASSP Bulletin, 102*(1), 58–84.
Keneally, M. (2015, December 29). Year in review: 13 biggest news stories of 2015. From crashes and shootings, to the pope's visit and a daring prison escape. ABC News. Retrieved August 31, 2022, from https://abcnews.go.com/US/year-review-13-biggest-news-stories-2015/story?id=35852690
King, J., Jr. (2009, January 7). Education: The difference between hope and despair. *Huffington Post.* Retrieved August 6, 2022, from https://www.huffpost.com/entry/education-the-difference_b_148855
Kingsbury, K. (2008, December 16). Will Arne Duncan shake up America's schools? *Time Magazine.* Retrieved August 25, 2022, from https://web.archive.org/web/20081217002156/http://www.time.com/time/nation/article/0,8599,1866783,00.html
Konik, A. (2014). Tentative rulings in California trial courts. *Columbia Journal of Law and Social Problems, 47*, 325–383. Retrieved August 13, 2022, from http://jlsp.law.columbia.edu/wp-content/uploads/sites/8/2017/03/47-Konik.pdf
Langer, E. (2016, March 31). Shirley Hufstedler, first secretary of the newly created Education Dept., dies at 90. *Washington Post.* Retrieved August 8, 2022, from https://www.washingtonpost.com/national/shirley-hufstedler-first-secretary-of-the-newly-created-education-dept-dies-at-90/2016/03/31/752ac8a0-f74f-11e5-8b23-538270a1ca31_story.html
Leung, R. (2004, January 6). The "Texas miracle." CBS News. Retrieved September 1, 2022, from https://www.cbsnews.com/news/the-texas-miracle/
Levoy, J. (2016, March 31). Shirley Hufstedler died at 90: The judge served as first secretary of education. *Los Angeles Times.* Retrieved August 8, 2022, from https://www.latimes.com/local/obituaries/la-me-shirley-hufstedler-20160401-story.html
Lindsay, J. M. (2018, December 20). Ten most significant world events in 2018. The Council on Foreign Relations. Retrieved August 31, 2022, from https://www.cfr.org/blog/ten-most-significant-world-events-2018
Loewus, L., & Sawchuk, S. (2014, July 4). NEA calls for Secretary Duncan's resignation. *Education Week.* Retrieved August 3, 2022, from https://www.edweek.org/leadership/nea-calls-for-secretary-duncans-resignation/2014/07
Marzell, T. L. (2018, January 24). Rod Paige: From classroom teacher to US superintendent of schools. Chalkboard Champions: Recognizing and Celebrating Great Teachers. Retrieved July 21, 2022, from https://chalkboardchampions.org/rod-paige-classroom-teacher-us-superintendent-schools/

Menas, A. (2021, February 3). 5 things we learned from Miguel Cardona's confirmation hearing. NEA News. Retrieved July 6, 2023, from https://www.nea.org/advocating-for-change/new-from-nea/what-we-learned-miguel-cardona-confirmation-hearing

Miller, J. (2016, December 12). The U.S. secretaries of education, a history, part I. The Educator's Room. Retrieved July 8, 2022, from https://theeducatorsroom.com/u-s-secretaries-education-history-part/

Miller, J. A. (1988, November 9). Cavazos: "I want to raise awareness" about the serious "education deficit." *Education Week*. Retrieved August 29, 2022. https://www.edweek.org/education/cavazos-i-want-to-raise-awareness-about-the-serious-education-deficit/1988/11

Miller, J. A. (1989, April 5). Cavazos, Lujan promise focus on Indian schools. *Education Week*. Retrieved November 5, 2022, from https://www.edweek.org/education/cavazos-lujan-promise-focus-on-indian-schools/1989/04

Miller, J. A. (1991, January 9). Educators hail nomination of Alexander as secretary. *Education Week*. Retrieved August 29, 2022, from https://www.edweek.org/education/educators-hail-nomination-of-alexander-as-secretary/1991/01

Mirga, T. (1982, September 12). Bell says panel's work confirms academic decline. *Education Week*. Retrieved July 10, 2022, from https://www.edweek.org/policy-politics/terrel-h-bell-second-u-s-education-secretary-biography-and-achievements/2017/08

National Assessment Governing Board (NAGB). (2020). Overview. Retrieved November 23, 2022, from https://www.nagb.gov/naep/about-naep.html

National Commission on Excellence in Education (NCEE). (1983). A nation at risk: The imperative for educational reform. A Report to the Nation and the Secretary of Education United States Department of Education. April 1983. Retrieved from https://edreform.com/wp-content/uploads/2013/02/A_Nation_At_Risk_1983.pdf

National Education Association. (2022). Take action. Retrieved August 1, 2022, from https://www.nea.org/advocating-for-change/action-center/take-action?

Nicosia, M. (2017, January 29). Phil-ing in: Meet the man overseeing America's schools while we wait for a new education secretary. The 74. Retrieved August 20, 2022, from https://www.the74million.org/article/phil-ing-in-meet-the-man-overseeing-americas-schools-while-we-wait-for-a-new-education-secretary/

Nolen, J. L., & Duignan, B. (2021, June 3). No Child Left Behind. *Encyclopedia Britannica*. https://www.britannica.com/topic/No-Child-Left-Behind-Act

Norris, M. (2005, April 7). Spellings: Flexibility on "No Child Left Behind." All Things Considered, National Public Radio. Retrieved August 3, 2022, from https://www.npr.org/2005/04/07/4581560/spellings-flexibility-on-no-child-left-behind

Olson, L. (1987, September 16). Bennett and the N.E.A.—a war of words. *Education Week*. Retrieved August 27, 2022, from https://www.edweek.org/education/bennett-and-the-n-e-a-a-war-of-words/1987/09

Olson, L., & Miller, J. A. (1991). The "education president" at midterm: Mismatch between rhetoric, results? Retrieved June 23, 2023, from https://www.edweek.org/education/the-education-president-at-midterm-mismatch-between-rhetoric-results/1991/01

Paige, R. (2002). An overview of America's education agenda. *Phi Delta Kappan, 83*(9), 708–713. Retrieved from https://doi.org/10.1177/003172170208300914.

Parker, N. W. (1978). *The president's cabinet and how it grew*. Parents' Magazine Press.

Peterson, P. (2022). In new book, Education Secretary Betsy DeVos emerges as a modern Alyosha. *Education Next, 22*(4). Retrieved December 1, 2022, from https://www.educationnext.org/hostages-no-more-school-choice-advances-farther-than-anticipated/

Philanthropy Roundtable. (2013, Spring). Interview with Betsy DeVos, the reformer. For years now, she has been at the forefront of the educational-reform movement. Retrieved August 30, 2022, from https://www.philanthropyroundtable.org/magazine/spring-2013-interview-with-betsy-devos-the-reformer/

Pitsch, M. (1990, October 3). Bush orders advisory panel on Hispanic education. *Education Week*. Retrieved August 28, 2022, from https://www.edweek.org/education/bush-orders-advisory-panel-on-hispanic-education/1990/10

Pratt, M. (2022, March 18). Lauro Cavazos, first Latino cabinet member dies. Associated Press. Retrieved November 25, 2022, from https://news.yahoo.com/lauro-cavazos-first-latino-cabinet-162955658.html

Radin, Beryl A., & Hawley, W. D. (1988). *The politics of federal reorganization: Creating the U.S. Department of Education*. Pergamon government and politics series. Pergamon Press.

Ravitch, D. (1983). *The troubled crusade: American education 1945–1980*. Basic Books.

Remembering 1991: The year in education. (1992, January 8). *Education Week*. Retrieved July 20, 2022, from https://www.edweek.org/education/remembering-1991-the-year-in-education/1992/01

Remembering 1992: The year in education. (1993, January 13). *Education Week*. Retrieved June 20, 2023, from https://www.edweek.org/education/remembering-1992-the-year-in-education/1993/01

Richard R. Riley Papers. (2018). South Carolina Political Collections. University of South Carolina, University Libraries. Retrieved August 13, 2022, from https://archives.library.sc.edu/repositories/6/resources/722

Richmond, K. (2017, January 17). Education advocates: DeVos lacks public school experience. CNN. Retrieved August 31, 2022, from https://www.cnn.com/2017/01/17/politics/betsy-devos-public-education-experience-cnntv/

Riley, R. W. (2000, March). The state of American education: Setting expectations. *Vital Speeches of the Day, 66*(11), 322. Retrieved from ProQuest One Academic.

Robelen, E. W. (2001, April 25). Paige announces plan to address mismanagement. *Education Week*. Retrieved November 6, 2022, from https://www.edweek.org/policy-politics/paige-announces-plan-to-address-mismanagement/2001/04

Roberts, S. (2016, March 31). Obituary of Shirley Hufstedler. *New York Times*. Retrieved August 2, 2022, from https://www.nytimes.com/2016/04/01/us/shirley-hufstedler-pioneering-judge-and-first-cabinet-level-education-secretary-is-dead-at-90.html

Rothman, R. (1988, February 17). Bennett asks Congress to put curb on "exploitative" for-profit schools. *Education Week*. Retrieved November 30, 2022, from https://www.edweek.org/education/bennett-asks-congress-to-put-curb-on-exploitative-for-profit-schools/1988/02

Sass, E. (2022). American education history timeline. Retrieved August 31, 2022, from https://eds-resources.com/educationhistorytimeline.html#2000

Shaw, S. (1986). Education secretary William Bennett's sweeping report on the nation's . . . UPI archives. Retrieved November 22, 2022, from https://www.upi.com/Archives/1986/09/02/Education-Secretary-William-Bennetts-sweeping-report-on-the-nations/1849526017600/

Smith, K. A. (2022, August 23). The Inflation Reduction Act is now law—here's what it means for you. Forbes Advisor. Retrieved August 31, 2022, from https://www.forbes.com/advisor/personal-finance/inflation-reduction-act/

Smyth, J. (1980, January 27). The education of Shirley Mount Hufstedler. *Washington Post*. Retrieved July 9, 2022, from https://www.washingtonpost.com/archive/lifestyle/1980/01/27/the-education-of-shirley-mount-hufstedler/53577ec5-9548-4ac4-86d5-ffa9f0bd60b6/

Spellings proposes changes to NCLB. (2008, April 23). *Washington Times*. Retrieved October 23, 2022, from https://www.washingtontimes.com/news/2008/apr/23/spellings-proposes-changes-to-nclb/

Spring, J. (2018). *The American school: From the Puritans to the Trump era* (10th ed.). Routledge Taylor & Francis Group.

Stafford, L. (2022, August 23). U.S. Education Secretary Cardona: How to fix teacher shortages, create safe schools. *Education Week*. Retrieved August 30, 2022, from https://www.edweek.org/policy-politics/u-s-education-secretary-cardona-how-to-fix-teacher-shortages-create-safe-schools/2022/08

Stallings, D. T. (2002). A brief history of the U.S. Department of Education: 1979–2002. *Phi Delta Kappan, 83*(9). Retrieved from https://doi.org/10.1177/003172170208300910

Stone, T. (2022, August 26). Education Secretary Miguel Cardona addresses legality of Biden's student loan handout program. Fox News interview with Miguel Cardona. Retrieved August 30, 2022, from https://www.realclearpolitics.com/video/2022/08/26/education_secretary_miguel_cardona_addresses_legality_of_bidens_student_loan_handout_program.html

Suarez, R. (2001, January 17). Richard Riley: The outgoing education secretary reflects on his experiences in the Clinton Cabinet. PBS NewsHour. Retrieved August 31, 2022, from https://www.pbs.org/newshour/show/richard-riley

Suglia, C. (2017, February 5). The Education Department is in good hands for now. Romper. Retrieved August 30, 2022, from https://www.romper.com/p/who-is-the-acting-secretary-of-education-phil-rosenfelt-is-a-career-employee-of-the-education-department-35623

Sweeney, L. (1981, March 26). Terrel Bell. *The Christian Science Monitor*. Retrieved August 22, 2022, from https://www.csmonitor.com/1981/0326/032654.html#

Thompson, C. (2013, August 26). "What are the Common Core State Standards?" Associated Press as reported by *U.S. News*. Retrieved December 1, 2022, from https://www.usnews.com/news/politics/articles/2013/08/26/what-are-the-common-core-state-standards?page=2

Thompson, E. (2021, May 27). History of online education. The technology boom of the mid-1980s is most remembered for the first personal computer, but that era also saw another important creation: online learning. The Best Schools. Retrieved August 31, 2022, from https://thebestschools.org/magazine/online-education-history/

Thorne, A. (2010, June). *U.S. Founding Fathers on education, in their own words*. National Association of Scholars. Retrieved August 12, 2022, from https://www.nas.org/blogs/article/u_s_founding_fathers_on_education_in_their_own_words

Toppo, G. (2017, January 9). Union head: Trump schools pick "the most anti-public-education nominee" in history. USA Today. Retrieved June 23, 2023, from https://www.usatoday.com/story/news/2017/01/09/union-head-trump-schools-pick/96357646/

Tosh, J. (2015). *The pursuit of history: Aims, methods, and new directions in the study of history* (6th ed.). Routledge.

Treon, C. (2022, August 26). Education Secretary Cardona: Student loan relief and Inflation Reduction Act "really cancels itself out," naysayers are unAmerican. Yahoo News. Retrieved August 31, 2022, from https://news.yahoo.com/education-secretary-cardona-student-loan-203911638.html

Turner, C. (2020, November 10). How Education Secretary Betsy DeVos will be remembered. National Public Radio. Retrieved August 30, 2022, from https://www.npr.org/2020/11/19/936225974/the-legacy-of-education-secretary-betsy-devos

Turner, C. (2021, March 1). Lifelong educator Miguel Cardona confirmed as education secretary. National Public Radio. Retrieved August 14, 2022, from https://www.npr.org/2021/03/01/972611847/lifelong-educator-miguel-cardona-confirmed-as-education-secretary

Turner, C., & Uzunlar, E. (2021, February 3). Education pick Miguel Cardona's message to lawmakers: "En la unión está la fuerza." *All Things Considered*, National Public Radio. Retrieved August 30, 2022, from https://www.npr.org/sections/biden-transition-updates/2021/02/03/963620575/education-pick-miguel-cardonas-message-to-lawmakers-en-la-union-esta-la-fuerza

Ujifusa, A. (2016, April 1). First-ever education secretary had a groundbreaking tenure at the department. *Education Week*. Retrieved July 30, 2022, from https://www.edweek.org/policy-politics/first-ever-education-secretary-had-a-groundbreaking-tenure-at-the-department/2016/04

UPI Archives. (1982, October 21). Education secretary Terrell Bell said Thursday a high-technology world . . . Retrieved August 26, 2022, from https://www.upi.com/Archives/1982/10/21/Education-Secretary-Terrell-Bell-said-Thursday-a-high-technology-world/7241404020800/

U.S. Constitution. (1776). Retrieved August 12, 2022, from https://constitutioncenter.org/the-constitution]

U.S. Department of Education. (n.d.). Arne Duncan, secretary of education—Biography. Retrieved August 31, 2022, from https://www2.ed.gov/news/staff/bios/duncan.html

U.S Department of Education. (n.d.). Betsy DeVos, secretary of education—Biography. Retrieved on August 22, 2022, from https://www2.ed.gov/news/staff/bios/devos.html?src=hp

U.S. Department of Education. (n.d.). John B. King, Jr., secretary of education—Biography. Retrieved August 31, 2022, from https://www2.ed.gov/news/staff/bios/king.html

U.S. Department of Education. (n.d.). Margaret Spellings, secretary of education—Biography. Retrieved August 31, 2022, from https://www2.ed.gov/print/news/staff/bios/spellings.html

U.S. Department of Education. (n.d.). Richard W. Riley, secretary of education. Retrieved August 31, 2022, from https://www2.ed.gov/offices/OS/riley.html

U.S. Department of Education. (n.d.). Rod Paige, secretary of education—Biography. Retrieved August 31, 2022, from https://www2.ed.gov/news/staff/bios/paige.html

U.S. Department of Education. (1991). America 2000: An education strategy. Sourcebook. May 1991.

U.S. Department of Education. (2009). About Ed/Offices. https://www2.ed.gov/about/offices/list/os/index.html

U.S. Department of Education. (2010). An overview of the U.S. department of education. Retrieved August 12, 2022, from https://www2.ed.gov/about/overview/focus/what_pg4.html

U.S. Department of Education. (2019, April 4). U.S. department of education: Secretary DeVos applauds consensus on higher education reforms. U.S. Security News Reports. Retrieved June 23, 2019, from https://americansecuritynews.com/stories/512406103-u-s-department-of-education-secretary-devos-applauds-consensus-on-higher-education-reforms

U.S. Department of Education. (2021a). Dr. Miguel Cardona, secretary of education—Biography. U.S. Department of Education. Retrieved August 30, 2022, from https://www2.ed.gov/news/staff/bios/cardona.html

U.S. Department of Education. (2021b). The federal role in education. U.S. Department of Education. Retrieved August 10, 2022, from https://www2.ed.gov/about/overview/fed/role.html

U.S. Department of Education. (2021c). Programs. Retrieved from https://webarchive.loc.gov/all/20201108154342/https://www2.ed.gov/programs/gtep/index.html

U.S. news | education. (2022, July 30). *USA Today*. Retrieved August 1, 2022, from https://www.usatoday.com/news/education/

USA Spending. (2022). Agency profile, Department of Education (ED). FY 2022 Summary. Retrieved July 31, 2022, from https://www.usaspending.gov/agency/department-of-education?fy=2022

Vik, P. (1984). A response to A Nation at Risk: More looking and less leaping. *NASSP Bulletin*, *68*(470), 53–59. https://doi.org/10.1177/019263658406847016

Vinovskis, M. A. (1999). National education goals panel. The road to Charlottesville: The 1989 education summit. Department of History, Institute for Social Research, and School of Public Policy. University of Michigan. Retrieved August 28, 2022, from https://govinfo.library.unt.edu/negp/reports/negp30.pdf

Volmer, J. (2021). Retrieved November 15, 2022, from https://www.jamievollmer.com/

West, P. (1994, May 18). Riley sees E.D. role in pushing use of technology. *Education Week*. Retrieved August 31, 2022, from https://www.edweek.org/technology/riley-sees-e-d-role-in-pushing-use-of-technology/1994/05

What happened in 1985–1988. (2022). The People's History Home. Retrieved June 23, 2023, from https://www.thepeoplehistory.com/1980s.html

White House. (2022). The cabinet. Retrieved August 12, 2022, from https://www.whitehouse.gov/administration/cabinet/

Zais, M. (2018). Official biography. Retrieved August 30, 2022, from https://dmacc.edu/news/Documents/MickZaisBio.pdf?ID=101

Zion Market Research. (2022). U.S. education market by type. *Zion Market Research*. Retrieved August 31, 2022, from https://www.zionmarketresearch.com/report/us-education-market

www.ingramcontent.com/pod-product-compliance
Lightning Source LLC
Chambersburg PA
CBHW021800230426
43669CB00006B/151